Born
Into
Chains

A Collection
Of Fragments and Poetry

Robert L. Angus

PART ONE

2008 - 2009

Preface

The first part of this collection was written between October 2008 and April of 2009. It was during this period in time that the author was living in Calgary, several months after his divorce. Alliances were shifting between friends and work associates, he had just purchased a company, and he had taken in a stray named N. who needed a roof over her head.

The writing from this period are fraught with angst of a man whose life is facing unpredictability, uncertainty, and who has suffered recent horrific losses.

Love seems distant and on the summit of an insurmountable mountain peak. The writing is dark, gloomy, painful. And yet, in the dark, there is some hope, some searching for meaning.

At the time of this writing, in the midst of April 2009, it is worthy to note that he is in a much better place in his life, with joy following in his wake.

Editor

New Mythology

Creating a new mythology
We watched the performance
Goddess worshipful
While standing in the crowd
Queen of the dark and the light
Holding tightly to each other
Perfectly ephemeral
While waves of sound passed over us
Sunlight dancing upon her brow
Our fingers intertwined like lace brocade
Wind sweeping hair across her cheek
Her leopard print dress
Goddess worshipful
I felt the sun rise again
Our Lady of Joy.

Ginsbergian Mythology
A New Mythology V.2

Crafting one virgin fable
Viewing an exhibition
Diva in excelsius
Positioned amongst the audience
Matron of the shadow and the flame
Each grasping finally to the other
Consummate evanescence
Recurring resonance reverberating
Shifting rays halo perfect forehead
Fingers tightly gripped in twain
Breeze folding hair across her face
Animal print draping her body
Diva in excelsius
Morning sun eclipsing horizon
Saintly woman of Glory.

Scribus di Illuminati
New Mythology - V.3

We designed upon the walls, and our hearts
The stories we experienced upon each page
The Lady of the Letter, the Exalted Word.
She watched as each story took form
The light flickering over the ink and vellum
Combining each phrase with excellent beauty
Carefully balanced against the other
Holy words echoing against hallowed chamber
Endless light flowing from within to without
Fingers and hearts annointed with prayer
Breath pronouncing sacred chants
And there she stood in flowing garments
The Lady of the Letter, the Exalted Word.
The light rising above its hidden state
The Woman Clothed with the Sun.

Eyes

I remember the first time I saw you,
a beautiful face amongst the crowd
You were there, wearing white
An angel hidden in a sea of madness.

You were examining my wares,
Challenging me with questions
Your eyes looking up at me
And I was taken in by you.

I assumed, like all days before,
That I would leave unfulfilled,
The angel's smile fading
Back into an ocean of faces.

I remember you when you arrived,
A smile of recognition,
I had memorized your features
In that brief moment.

You were beautiful, polite, friendly.
It was your birthday,
Though I was not to find that out
Until much later.

You came again, a week and a day later,
Spending time with me while I worked,
Taking in what I did,
From moment to blessed moment.

I enjoyed your spirit,
I was filled with the light
That you carry within you,
And felt blessed to know you.

We have spoken each day since,
And I am always amazed by you.
So precious do I find these
Many wonderful words we share.

I am amazed by you,
And I feel blessed,
To spend time with you,
Dear Lady, thank you.

Everything That I Know of Love

Dedicated to Alison Davis

Everything that I know of Love
You have helped me to understand.
You were there when I lost everything,
You held my head, you held my hand.

You heard me over the telephone,
And while I grieved, you listened.
I spoke in earnestness about my pain,
You did not grow weary or hasten.

You listened to me with joyful giving,
You did not try to sway me with words.
You merely opened your heart to my story,
You gave meaning each time you heard.

You helped me to open my eyes,
And appreciate all that I went through,
Everything that I know about love,
I learned from listening to you.

A year has passed and even now,
You listen with kindness to all I relate,
Even if you are busy with your own life,
And a million miles away.

You were always there with me,
Within me, and all around,

You taught me to love, dear friend,
Without ever making a sound.

A Dream

I had a dream about you last night. It was a good dream, filled with light and love, joy and unity.

I had a dream that our lives were fulfilled in every way, that we overcame our challenges with happiness to have learned a new lesson, and to add to our skills, lovingly and with patience.

I had a dream that we got along perfectly, with respect to each others' dreams and wishes, our desires and our passions intermingling like two heartbeats in a beautiful rhythm.

I had a dream that we were married in the sun under the trees, the slow gentle breeze rustling the canopies above us, your hair made perfectly against your dress.

I had a dream that we built our house together, choosing the furniture, the paints, the location, and everything we needed to suit our needs.

I had a dream that our children were happy, playing together in our yard while we watched them, played with them, helped them with their homework, worked with them on their projects.

I had a dream that we vacationed in the various places in the world that we've always wanted to see - the temples in India, the mountains in Peru, the Louvre in Paris, the vineyards in France, the desert tribes in the Sahara.

I had a dream that we were wealthy in our own way, that our income took care of ourselves and those we loved, so no one would feel the pressure of never having enough.

I know that all of this is possible, and that love will guide us there, one day, somehow.

Know that I love you, and that life will happen the way we choose it to, slowly, and with measured steps towards our dreams. This dream is mine, and you fit in it, because your dreams are yours, and like a jigsaw puzzle, we can find all the pieces to make it right.

God Willing.

Chapter Once

Finally, I found myself finishing school, after what seemed months of toil avoiding the cafeteria and its hour long card games, only to fail and have to make up the classes I skipped to play there. 114 classes missed, the majority of the year, spent in the cafeteria eating donuts and drinking old coffee, avoiding my teachers and the truancy officer. I had received only two credits for the semester for my teaching airbrushing to the other students in my graphics design course, and the other classes, though I missed most of them, I was ready to pass the examinations and get at least a passing grade.

My teachers didn't really understand the point of even taking the tests, but I made up my classes on a two for one option, giving up lunch hours and an hour each evening, sitting in home-room, reading my text books and studying. There really was no point - I already understood nuances in Shakespeare that my teacher's didn't get, and had finished the mathematics semester within a month of starting it. Public school only teaches higher quality students to ignore authority and avoid discipline, what need is there to make an arrival in class only to remain bored, having a professor talk down to you because you're not paying attention? I got more students in trouble than not, if only because I was so far ahead of the class that I was more of a bother to the teachers because I was always goofing off and messing around.

So, my second time around grade ten, I had finally made it through to examination week, and was studied enough to pass the grade, if only I could show up to the exams. (Even in college, I was often the first person out of the door, and usually with one of the highest grades in the class).

As was usual, I was to be found outside of the school, smoking cigarettes near the parking lot, outside of the drama class doors with the other nicotine addicts. We didn't bother leaving the school grounds to smoke, even though to be caught meant certain punishment - usually cleaning the bathrooms with a muddy mop-bucket and a grungy towel that smelled mysteriously like urine and mildew.

My mother was rarely aware that I was missing so many classes, as we didn't have a home phone, and the automatic calls which the school computer made to parents of wayward children were never answered or returned. I'm sure that somewhere there is a CIA/CSIS file that lays out my gift for avoiding my educational responsibility and for my overall tardiness and undignified behavior towards school authority, but I spent my time there nonetheless.

Two days before exams, and I was finishing up my last make-up class, a feeling of joyful accomplishment filling my lungs with cries of enthusiasm as well as the reefer my friends had lit in celebration. This was the boring as shit weed that circulated high school drug culture in the early nineties, not the break-neck super-pot grown by the government that turns modern high school students into super-genius nymphoids ready to take on the world.

Liber Niger Solis

Ten Universes seen and unseen
Reflected in the known and the unknown.
You experience all of these simultaneously
But are unaware of them unanimously.
The world of your senses hide them:
This is what you know as "occult".

These worlds are affected by extrordinary senses.
These worlds are opened only to the casual observer
Through the use of hallucinatory drugs or trace
These worlds are not available to the body of your senses
But can be affected by the dream state of the shaman
Or the ritual of the Sorcerer, or the prayers of the Priest.

All that you see, touch, hear, taste, smell, and feel
Are the tangible symbols of these ten worlds
Experienced by the body, and translated to the mind
In a manner unexposed to what you call "reality".
The common animal will never experience the ten worlds.
The task of the enlightened is to seek them out,
To make oneself aware of them in his daily excursions,
To learn to manipulate and control them,
And thereby place oneself above them,
From a place originally below.

The mind of the animal cannot reconcile these worlds
With the world of his daily experience.
Madness may follow as one gets lost amongst these worlds.
Is it madness, or awareness?

Can one balance on the edge of a knife point
In hopes of keeping his wits about him?
The answer is no.
There is no sanity for those who abstain from the norm.
Once aware, always aware. Once blind, always blind.
There is no difference.

Painted Days

I am reminded of painted days
Our faces bright in summer halos
Of the time shared in tenderness
And think of you each day you're gone
Hoping that you'll return safely.

Last night we shared a dance
Ignoring guests with dinner
Disregarding their questions
To spend time with each other
Crafting psalms for angelic voices.

I held your hand as we danced
As if for the first time realizing
How wonderful it is to love you
How grateful I am to know you
How joyful it is to be with you.

You laughed when I called you, "Goddess"
Understand that I am humbled by you
That I invoke you in my mind,
That I sing praises to you,
That I worship you for who you are
And nothing more.

I am reminded of painted days
On the canvas of my memory

Of the times we shared in tenderness
Our faces bright with the glow
Of shared moments.

Once upon a time...

We were friends. I saw you, and knew that I couldn't have you in an ordinary world. I dreamed of you. I spoke to you in my sleep. I spoke to pictures of you and knew that, if I said the right things, did the right things, that we could be together. I knew, and so it was. We had a great friendship. The kind of friendship that they make movies out of. We had a closeness that was passionate, a seduction that went beyond sex and more deeply into the tissue of our beings. We were connected in a spiritual way. We could feel each other from across the country, speaking to each other in our minds, holding each other in spirit. Constantly we were drawn together, our touch tender and loving, speaking more with our love than we could have with words. There were worlds in an instant when we hugged, the smell of your hair filling my nostrils, becoming the only sense I could experience. There was heaven in that moment. My eyes filled with tears every time I held you. You were my everything in that moment. Such a terrible thing to manifest, because when I lost you, I became nothing. To lose everything is such a terrible price to pay for a relationship. I lost myself in you. I had nothing left when you went away. I cannot make that mistake again. I cannot make that mistake. I cannot.

And yet, here I am again, falling in love with another woman, creating a bond just as strong, just as spiritual, just as loving, but without the magic that I used to draw you to me. Is it pure? Perhaps. Is it love? Definitely. Is it real? Only time can tell. But it will not be my everything. I cannot risk my mind and soul like that again. It is too terrible a price.

I look back on our friendship and I wonder - if I could have held on to that moment, would it have been worth it? Or would you have gone the way you went anyways?

From a Prince to a King

There was a time when we woke up together in the morning, and got ready for the day. My wife would put on coffee while I took a shower and the kids got dressed for school. They made their lunches and found their homework, and we would make breakfast together. Often, we would make something special, and then we'd get the puppies ready for their walk and go to the school together. After hugs and kisses, we would part ways, and my wife, youngest daughter and I would walk the puppies along the ridge overlooking the river, maybe even taking a quick trip down the ravine to see the waterfalls. It was always a magical experience.

We'd get home and make love, the cool air blowing in through the window, and after we relaxed together in the glow of the sun peaking over the trees in the park through the windows, we would get dressed and drive to work together.

The trip was always filled with singing and laughter, she was always dressed beautifully, her hair radiant against the sun light. We'd talk about the day, and take a quick stop at our favorite coffee shop before walking back to our store. We held hands as we went, our daughter skipping along beside us. She was always the star attraction each morning at the coffee shop. She loved her hot chocolate, while we enjoyed our Americano's and discussed the talk of the day with our friends.

We'd get to work, and I'd start binding the next order while she left to take care of business, making sales calls to our clients, daughter in tow, and drive across town to deliver completed orders or pick up much needed supplies.

The days would flow by quickly, and we'd meet together again at the day's end and make dinner together. The kids would finish their homework, bathe, and get ready for bed. I'd read to them, sitting on the floor in the hallway while my wife sat near my, sewing, drawing, or listening with her head on my lap. Eventually they'd all fall asleep, and we'd retire to the dining room to discuss the day, talk about our friends, plan out our week, or finish up some work that we'd left undone.

The evening was often spent together like this, a fire burning, flickering twinkling lights reflecting against the front room windows. We'd often share a bottle of wine and fall asleep in each other's arms, naked bodies pressed tight against each other, her hands caressing my arms which were wrapped closely around her.

My life was heaven, once upon a time.

Fairie tales are written backwards, which is why they seem so unreal. They end with a happily ever after, following a challenge overcome, and a calm, happy beginning...once upon a time, long long ago.

The reality is that life begins as a struggle, our parents educate us into believing that if we work hard, that everything will work out. Suddenly, a dragon rears its ugly head. The stories never tell you how terrified the characters are, they never relate the gut wretching fear that immobilizes the mind and makes decisions difficult. The stories lie. Finally, after the enemy wins, takes the princess, and banishes the prince, and after his life has crumbled around him, she lives on with the wicked monster, who gives her a fanciful life of luxury (because we all know dragons have a hoard of treasure hidden somewhere). Their children are spread across a wasteland of fear and confusion, their diaspora forgotten against the splendor of the treasures the dragon showers her with.

The prince is not yet a wise man, he has not learned the lessons of life yet, he has not built a temple within himself yet. He is untested, impure, and unrighteous. He must learn to defeat his inner dragons, before he can ever defeat the outer ones. The prince is immature, he is greedy, he is easily angered. The prince has magic within him, and he uses it often, without ever realizing that the magic he has harnessed is raw, impure, and undistilled. He has not yet realized that the magic he uses is wild, and untamed, and that the only way to tame it is through the path of the wizard, which is a dark and lonely path indeed. The prince fears this path, even though he knows that it is inevitable, it is his destiny, and fate will lead him there, thrashing, kicking and screaming if necessary. The more the prince fights the path chosen for him, the harder it will be. Sacrifice and Surrender are the only requirements. All he has will be stripped from him, so that he will learn how to harness the magic within for the good of all. That is the only way he can become a true leader, a ruler of men, a conqueror of the self.

I've since had wise women tell me that I'm still a prince, better off for having lost the princess to the dragon, and my children are with relatives who care about them. But alas, I am still banished, forever knowing that my fairy tale life is at an end, and that fairy tales are not real, are never real, and only exist inside of books and the delusional minds of people who want to believe that the world is indeed a good and wonderful place.

I have no fairy tales left. The magic is gone, my magic mirror shattered against the flag stones of some foreign castle which holds my princess captive in a gilded cage of her own choosing. She is happy - that is all that matters to her, and her children, she believes, are better off without their father, without their home, without the family they once had.

Was the prince really so bad? Princes are, by nature, arrogant and charming. They are always saving the princess from the dangers that princesses are ere to.

I live in a dungeon, one which houses my workshop - much like the secret magical manors of the wizard who would teach the prince to buck up and get over the tragedy of their lives. Yes, son, the magic you once experienced is real, but in order to control it, you must first learn to control yourself.

The wizard takes the prince by the hand, leads him to a life of poverty, silence, and loneliness, his heart ever yearning for a taste of the life that once was. But he also teaches him to turn lead into gold, the figurative quest of self perfection. This quest alone may take many lifetimes, and in time, the prince forgets the love that once held him to a superficial princess whose love for a dragon will ultimately be her doom.

In time, the prince will awaken from his self imposed life of darkness and return to the light. His inner light will glow for all to see, and the abundance that he once had in a fairy tale will be controlled in the same way that he has learned to control his own self, his mind, his world. He will learn that the life he once tasted was only a dream, not intended to last forever, and that it was only a single string on the instrument of his life. He will, through the trial of his inner sphinx, have learned that To Know, To Dare, To Will, and To Keep

Silence is the key to understanding that one string will only ever play a simple tune, but that understanding all of the strings, he will make a beautiful music of his life, and the sounds which he makes are magical, the words a greater spell than the one he had cast before.

Magic is. Love is.

The prince becomes a king.

To M.K.

I saw you last night and my heart broke
To see the lows to which you have fallen.
I watched as your unhappiness
Blurred the lines of your face
Sullen and dirtied by your fears
Broken hopes and ravaged dreams
Pitiful sadness in your eyes.

I wanted to love you, once.
All I see in you is the alcohol,
The binge drinking sweats
And the morning headaches
Wondering where you were
The night before
When all of this happened.

I used to think of us,
What it would be like to hold you,
And now all I see is the darkness
Of what may never be,
What must never be -
The painful nights of wondering
Where you are, and who you're with,
If you're safe, and if you'll come home.

I saw you last night
And my heart went out to you,
You hugged me, begging me
To be there for you

When you came down.
But I cannot be there.
I cannot put my family though this.
Instinctively, you yearn for meaning
In a world where meaning is bottled
Behind a bar, dished out in ounces.

I wanted to be with you,
But you know and I know
That it will never be.
You want me to save you,
But I am tired of saving people,
I am a victim of my own concerns.
I have my own life to live,
My own life to fight with,
My own problems and terrors.
I have my own path,
And I must travel it
Without you.

Good Gossip Gone Gaga

Intervention? Hilarious.
Laugh at your own disease
Before bringing your drama
To my door.

My poverty came
On the heel of an opportunity
To grow my business two steps forward,
One step back.

Sorry to disappoint you,
I am not the person who
Takes kindly to gossip,
No matter how well intended.

Doctor,
Heal thyself.
I do not need
Your cure.

You want to help?
Let hollow friendships die
Because friends do not gather
In conspiracy against another.

I held your hand
When you were depressed,
I held you when you
Were unsure.

What you learned,
From what my heart endured,
Was to kick a man
When he is down.

You would gather
Behind closed doors
To make a list of wrongs--
Never to hear my side.

I do not need your prescription--
I examined my heart
And found it wanting --
You should do the same.

I walked out on you,
I wished you a good life
Because I did not want
To be a part of it.

I don't need your advice --
I have been to those places
That you have only feared
To tread

I learned to do with
What I have,
And to survive,
Where others fail.

I know that
The higher the climb
The greater the view
From the top.

Just remember:
It was not me
Gathering to talk
About you.

How much
Honor
Is there
In explaining it?

Note:

Consider the source when meddling in the lives and affairs of others. In both cases, these are women I have been involved with. In both cases, these are women I have detached from. There is some hurt there, but that does not make their rationality any more defensible, nor does it make them right.

Intervention Cancelled

I am not an alcoholic.
I am not a drug addict.
I don't beat my kids.
I am not a gambler.

I am not going to listen to your list of things that you think I've done wrong.

This passive aggressive attack on my character is reaching idiotic proportions.

I'm sure that you believe that your intentions are good, but I'm afraid that your method is flawed. If you had a real problem with me, then I expect you to be honest enough with me to come to me and tell me. If it is something that I agree needs changing, then I will listen, as I have before. Ganging up on a person, calling his friends and asking them to help you with your list is no better than character assassination.

Can I be invited to another intervention? Cause this is fun. Really.

Note:

I am addicted to writing notes, if only because it keeps me relatively sane. Think, what would I be like if I bottled everything up and didn't explore my thoughts and feelings in a written media? I'd likely be angry, frustrated, and far less successful than I am right now. (Gosh, that would suck!)

Karel, as I said before, if the problem was a real one, someone would have come forth and we could have chatted about it. An intervention is staged for a person who has a serious condition, not for an ex girlfriend who has a problem with me and wants to voice her concerns in a place where her friends can back her up and make her feel like she's being listened to. That goes for Erinn as well.

As my priest and my other friends have already mentioned, they were not going to be involved because it sounded "petty". I'm disappointed that you hadn't selected one friend to chat with me, in a reasonable and friendly manner.

Calling up a group of friends to "intervene" is ridiculous -- what was the ultimatum that you as a group were going to offer, that I see counseling or you'd all shun me? For what, not being around when Angie wanted me to be? Or was it that I wouldn't sleep with her anymore? Or perhaps it was that I wasn't around to clean, because I was helping Melanie move all weekend?

Really, when you think about it, I moved out because she was dumping her drama on me, and I wasn't about to put up with it. I will not put up with abuse in any form, emotional, verbal, or financial.

In addition, were the group of you really "friends" then I might actually think that you'd have had the respect to come to me with your problems individually, instead of trying to make it a group effort.

Do you realize that an intervention is a "LAST CHANCE" option? Its emotional blackmail. Its an ultimatum. "Change or else..." What you are proposing is a cheap shot at making yourselves feel good by making sure that a person who is already climbing out of a hole knows that they're in a hole in the first place. You are not offering solutions, you are voicing your accusations as a group, so that your victim doesn't have a chance to reply in a fair or reasonable manner.

If ten people throw one accusation each, it is up to the accused to defend himself ten times. Rather exhausting, I'd say. And coercive.

If any of you are social engineers, then great, sign me up. But as it stands, half of the group in question suffers from debilitating psychological problems, and the other half empower them to continue with their manipulative and overly dramatic behavior.

I wash my hands of it.

As it is, these people do not realize that I have had and lost so many times in my life that it is not something abnormal. I have become one of the most resourceful people I know because of it. I don't need anyone in particular to feel good about my life. I am a good person, and I don't need another's pat on the back to tell me so. If a person is going to judge me, that is their problem, it tells me more about who they are than it tells me about who I am.

As I told Angie when I left her place the last time, I am one of the most accomplished people I know. I may have hit a down-turn in my life economically, but that doesn't mean that I am down for the count, it means that I am on an up-turn in the cycle, and the next crescendo is HUGE...

As I've mentioned before, I am always into hearing what people have to say -- one on one. If someone perceives a problem with me, I will listen to their thoughts, and take their advice into consideration. If I perceive it as inaccurate, I'll usually laugh it off with a joke and move along.

A friend spoke to me yesterday, and his words were, "I'm not worried about you, Robert. I know you'll come through this okay. If there's anyone I have faith in, its you."

The Interventioners

"Ben has a problem. He's X."

"Really?"

"Yeah, have you noticed?"

"A little, yeah."

"Well, I don't like that he's X-ing. I think we should call up everyone he knows and see if they have noticed him X-ing, too."

"You call Bob, Bill, Fred, Sara, Shane, Tom, Dick, Harry, Wilma, Wilfred, Anne, and I'll call Jeff, Shiela, Matthew, Mark, Luke, John, and Earl."

...
...
...

(Sample Conversation)

"Hey, Bob, have you noticed that Ben's been X-ing a lot lately?"

"Er, no, not really. Why, is he?"

"Yeah, he is. I think we should do something about it."

"Well, if its as bad as you think it is, then yeah. And while we're at it, lets bring up his Y-ing as well."

"Yeah, I don't like that he Y's all the time either."

"Well, hey, lets call up some of his other friends and we'll have a meeting and talk about it."

"Sounds good."

...

...

...

"Bob, Bill, Fred, Sara, Shane, Tom, Dick, Harry, Wilma, Wilfred, Anne, Jeff, Shiela, Matthew, Mark, Luke, John, and Earl, we're here to discuss Ben's X and Y habit. Is there anything else you think we should be discussing?"

"Er, yeah, Ben did W, and I saw him doing too much V and U as well."

"It really annoys me when Ben is being all T and S."

"Ben is too R. And he's really Q, too."

"Ben is into O,P..."

"Yeah, and L, M, N, etc..."

(When the gossip session ends, a smaller group of "interveners" is selected to represent the group and confront Ben with their concerns, A through Z.)

Quick Interview

How do you view yourself?

I am ambitious. I won't be happy with second best, but will go through second to get to first. I may not have what I want right now, but I am patient and willing to work towards my ideals, my goals. I am learning the hard way. I am learning every moment of every day. Attaining my goals is like learning a skill - I will learn a bit more every day. I am committed to learning more every day. Just so, I will reach my goal by spending some time every day reaching for them, moving towards them, inch by inch. I am already one of the most accomplished people I know, and I have faith that the Universe will provide to those who help themselves.

What type of girlfriend are you looking for?

I like to enjoy myself with people, but get bored easily. I despise drama, can't stand to be around negative people. I like social situations, and I love to flirt. As much as I would like to commit to someone, they have to be the very best of the very best to keep me interested. If there are any personality flaws, then I'm afraid its just not going to last longer than a few weeks. I'm picky. Now, that's not to say that I don't have flaws, I do, and I am an asshole, if only because I don't put up with other people's shit and abuse. I'm probably the only person in the world what idolizes Melvin Udall, and Gordon Gecko. I'm a villian, if that's what you need me to be. But I'm also a really nice guy. I can say "I love you" and mean it. I can also say it to please you, because thats what you want to hear. I can also say it as a way to get what I want. (Is this me being honest here!???? Look up who Melvin Udall and Gordon Gecko are...)

Do you think that you are ready for a relationship?

If she is amazing. I don't mean sexually (though that definitely helps), but intellectually stimulating, sexy, fun, relaxed, positive, committed, talented, supportive, outgoing, and "The Best"...as my ex wife used to say, "Perfect for me".

How serious are you about love?

Er...I love unconditionally, if not permanently.

What are your views on education?

Education is very important, but knowledge is completely useless without the direction of a goal, a master plan to work towards, and the willingness to be absolutely dedicated and persevere until that goal is reached.

What is the right job for you?

I am doing my perfect career. I love what I do, it satisfies all of my goals and creative desires.

How do you view success?

Success is the creating, planning, execution, completion, replacing, and then teaching of a goal. Set your goals HIGH...really HIGH...attain them. When someone says "What would you do with all that money?" when I tell them that I will earn $10 Million dollars a year, my answer is "More than you will." Will you ever fund a school for the bereft? Would you ever fund an orphanage for children in a third world country? Would you ever create libraries for the unfortunate? Would you ever build hospitals to help the sick? Would you like to single handedly fund the science behind a great medical discovery? Every man and Every Woman is a Star. Some only let their light shine dimly and give themselves excuses to fail.

What are you most afraid of?

The unknown. I let it get me for 5 seconds, then I let it go. Fear is inevitable, but it does not need to own you, it only needs to drive you harder forwards.

Okay, now, who is your true self?

Scared. Lonely. But constantly working to remedy that fact.

Supradramatis - Flash Fiction

She texted him while he was on his way to his friend's house, "We need to talk."

Bored of the exaggerated emotionalism he'd come to associate with her, he replied, "Sure, what's up?"

"You left the lid on the toilet up again. It splashes germs all over the bathroom."

"Er..." He typed back, wondering why this was so important as to be worth texting over.

"And you left a dish on the counter by the sink. There's a cup with dried milk in it. And a bowl. And garbage all over the floor of the kitchen. And, did you shower with my sweater in the tub?! It looks like you didn't even move it when you were in there last"

He reflected on these answers, in fact, pondered their significance in the grand scheme of his life. "I'm not even going to quantify that with an answer." He thought to himself. The thing that bothered him the most was that he did put the seat down on the toilet. He may have forgotten about it once in a while, I mean, the whole thing is a social cliche for a reason, but he did make it a point to pee sitting down, just so that there was no splashing of germs. "Gawd!", he muttered under his breath. Then he thought about the last night he slept there, when he'd slept on the couch so as not to give her the impression that they were going to get back together. They'd slept together twice since they broke up, and both times he stated that he was wearing clothes to keep them honest. She wanted to be cuddled, he was more than happy to oblige.

"You know, I think this is about something else. My phone is about to die, we'll talk tomorrow." He was just arriving at his friend's place, and texted back as an afterthought, "Look, I'll get my stuff out of your apartment tomorrow."

The evening went along well enough, his phone died and he gave it no further thought.

The next day, he had a meeting, and decided that he'd pick up his stuff after dinner. Unfortunately, dinner ran to midnight. So be it, he'll get it all out to the alley and spend an hour or two moving it the three blocks to his own place. If he was lucky, she'd be sound asleep and he could leave her keys in the mail box.

No such luck. She was sitting in the dark, furious, eyes blazing in the light of the computer.

"I'll get the majority of my things out right away."

"Its late."

"I know, it won't take long."

"Ill get help bringing it over this weekend. I want you out of my house."

"Um, look, I don't really know what to say to you. First off, I took your sweater out of the tub when I went to have a shower. I didn't know what you were doing with it, and I didn't want to wreck it, so I took it out. I put it back in after rinsing the tub out. As to the toilet, er, sorry. I thought I was putting the seat down. About the garbage in the kitchen, well, I really have no idea what you're talking about. My best friend was here with me when I left, and she doesn't remember seeing any garbage, either. About the dishes?

Well, I'm sorry, I had to go to work and didn't think to wash them before I left. My bad."

She glared at him, "I want my keys back."

"Sure, after I get my things out of your place. It shouldn't take long."

She raised her voice, "Get out NOW!"

"Um, look, I'm not yelling, I'm not cursing, and I'm not raising my voice at you. You're doing all three. I think you need to calm down."

"I don't trust you in my house. I don't feel safe here with you in my house. GET OUT! I want my keys back, NOW!" Her voice raised to an irrational shrillness that spoke of some serious nerve that had been touched once too many times in a past far beyond his involvement.

"Look, I'm not giving you my keys back until I get my things out of here. You don't trust me, and I don't trust you due to that same lack of trust. It goes both ways, I'm afraid."

"I'll call the police to escort you out of here. I don't trust you."

"Go ahead."

She dialed a mutual friend instead, and complained to her that he was moving out in the middle of the night, and that she didn't trust him, and that he was an asshole, and that he wasn't willing to give the keys back, and and and...

The accusations continued to fly at him like a swarm of bees, intended to do as much damage as possible. He said not a word, ignoring the angsty female on the couch and continued to pack his belongings out.

"Look, I really don't know what you're on about." he said, calmly, " I think you're being overly dramatic and your accusations and insults are irrational."

"You're the irrational one. And you're a liar. I know, because you said that your best friend has a crush on you, and I asked her and she said that she doesn't. I talked to mutual friends and they said the same thing, that you play games."

"You know, I think you're putting two different conversations together and taking them both out of context to fit your delusion. I remember saying that she's like a girlfriend, but without the sex. I also remember saying that I wouldn't get into a relationship with her because I've watched too many of her relationships blow up on her, and I don't want to be one of them. I wouldn't want to risk our friendship that way. And If I said that I think she has a crush on me, it doesn't mean she does, only that I THINK she dies. That doesn't make me a liar, at worst it makes me delusional. She's my best friend. Besides, who are these mutual friends?"

"Oh, you know, They and Them."

He pondered this with a little humor. They and Them, for lack of a better word, had been trying to get between She and He for over a month now, talking behind His back and telling her to break it off with Him. They also had a bit of a history, which its better not to get into right now, he thought. He had messed around with They, and Them had a crush on his best friend. They had even expressed how disappointed she was with Them, in spite of the fact that They was the one messing around in the first place. Ah, the plot thickens.

46

"Its not worth the argument," he thought, "You can't reason with an emotional person."

He handed her the keys. "Have a nice life." He uttered as he closed the door.

Publishing

There are three simple areas: Editing, Publishing, and Marketing.

We are going to assume, for the time being, that you have taken care of the Editing part, that is, its written, its edited, the layout has been formatted, cover is designed, and test copies have been printed. For all intents and purposes, we're ready to go.

The process of book publishing is fairly straight forward. Find a printer and binder to take the computer files you have created (should be in PDF format) and pay them to give you some finished books.

Ta Da! Done!

Oh, waitaminit, you want more?

You only need the following if you want to be in bookstores:

In Canada,you would to the National Library for an ISBN number. Later, you will have to send them two copies of your books to be archived. You can also register your copies with the Copyright office, and you're done. The national library will give you an ISBN number for your book and you will likely have to get an EAN bar code made from your ISBN number for the cover. Chain Bookstores won't take your books unless you have this number, as that is how they keep track of things.

In the United States, you would send copies to the Library of Congress after buying an ISBN number, and then put this information in the front of your book (along with the aforementioned EAN bar code).

Register your book with BOWKERS books in print, that way people can search directories to see that it exists.

Now, technically, you've published your book. Generally, a publishing house will take care of all of these legal aspects of book publishing, letting you get on you way to collecting royalty cheques and writing your next best seller.

The trick here, is that you are also going to need to market your book so that people can see them, and hopefully, buy them. That's the business part of this publishing gig.

Marketing Plan for Book Publishing - Part One

I am not a fan of the traditional publishing model. It is nepotistic and does not function in the current market of mainstream media. It doesn't work for the average person who wants to publish their books, and it limits what might be said by limiting the playing field to "what sells to the majority", or the average. Such mediocre standards creates mediocre writing, as well as a mass market media that only feeds the common herd what it wants to hear. Its tragic, really.

The majority of publishers use a model similar to this one (with some variation from company to company):

Commission a writer to write a book - or go through a slush pile of manuscripts and prospects until one pops out at the editor.

Pay the writer to produce the work in as short a time as possible, as cheaply as possible.

Send out a press release to any media willing to use the copy to fill space. Usually, the company that uses the press release is also a subsidiary owned by the company which owns a large share in the publishing house producing the book.

Pass the word on to the jobbers and sales people who work for the warehousers and distributors. They may or may not actually bother to actively promote the book, but some kickbacks help here, too. Bribery is great. As well, put a full page advertisement in your own catalogue to help promote the book to the booksellers who actually read such things.

Print unedited copies and send them to reviewers. This book still has typos and hasn't yet been picked apart by the editors. Its raw, but gives the reviewers something to read and comment upon. It also helps to build up the book's reputation.

While the book is being edited, formatted, and the cover is being designed, the legalities are taken care of (ISBN, etc).

Finally, the book is sent to the printers. Typically, a short print run of 2000 - 5000 copies is produced in hardcover and distributed to the warehouses and through them to the distributors.

Sometimes, they host a book launch with some razzle dazzle, and send the writer on a tour of a few cities and book stores to meet the public and hawk the book at signings and readings, as well as interviews and seminars, if they are applicable. If you can get onto Oprah, so much the better, but don't hold your breath, she only takes books that are produced by her head company's favorite subsidiaries.

Finally, it is hoped that, if the book is actually worth the paper its printed on, that the first printing sells out and it goes to a paperback publisher.

Now, at this point, the publisher has also sold the licensing of the book to other companies - film rights, audio-book rights, reprint rights, foreign printing rights, foreign language rights, serial rights to papers and magazines, and anywhere else that they can make some money on it.

If the book sells out, then they reprint it a few times until the glitz and glamour wears off, and they move on to the next big thing. In fact, the reality is that everyone except your publicist has moved on from the job seconds after the manuscript left the slush pile to begin with.

In some cases, they may even bother to have you sign a couple hundred copies for special sales and celebrities who might actually crack the cover.

Periodically, if the book has a lasting popularity, then the reprint rights are given over to another, smaller publishing house, who makes a pocket book version to sell a few copies here and there.

Ultimately, if the book doesn't sell worth a damn, then its covers are torn off and its returned to the warehouse, who returns it to the publisher, who cancels the contract. This means that the book has been "pulped". Nowadays, the book is "remaindered", meaning that the bookstore just drops the price every couple of weeks, and gives the publisher an ultimatum that "If you don't pulp the books and give us a credit, we'll just sell them at cost. If we can't get rid of them that way, we'll sell them at below cost, and you'll still owe us a credit for what we didn't make up. We know its not fair, but you dumped this trash on us to begin with."

Have you ever gone to your local big-box bookstore and seen a sticker on a book that said "10% off" or "price reduced"? Thats a remainder. Anything in the bargain bin is also a remainder, but sometimes these are just damaged or misprinted books that no one else wants.

So, thats the current business model. Its been the same for about sixty years, and isn't likely to change. Book publishing is a big money business, so its no surprise that most of the big media companies are owned by seven conglomerates. There may be hundreds of companies out there, but ultimately, most of them are owned by a very few big corporations, and these are in turn run by accountants who rule the editors.

Publishing used to be fun. It used to be done for the love of the book - for the love of literature - for the love of the craft. There was once nothing more sexual, nothing more seductive for a publisher, than to have that first copy off the press, open its sweet pages, and smell the fresh, wet ink, still warm off the page. Absolutely sexual, have no doubt.

Marketing Plan for Book Publishing - Part Two

Now we get into the books that don't get picked out of the slush pile.

There used to be a time when an author wrote a book, made a few copies by typing up to seven double-spaced sheets with a corresponding number of carbon paper sheets between, and sent them off to genre specific publishers, fingers crossed, with the hope of receiving the highly coveted advance cheque. The greatest fear of the writer was the inevitable, and often crushing rejection letter, as devoid of heart as it was devoid of any advice on how to make it better. If the writer was poor, then he or she would type these copies out themselves. They were never returned, so often it was a wasted effort.

Funding these projects was quite a task as well, because the production costs were so high. Type was often set by hand, or by a linotype machine (still, basically set by hand), and the printing plates cast in copper or lead. These matricies were set into the machines by hand, and a few thousand copies produced, collated by hand, bound by hand, and boxed up and shipped by hand. Finding investors was a task in itself, because the nature of the business is such that, often, the books would not sell very well, and the books may end up pulped or in the bargain bins.

In the late 1800's, it was popular to have short press runs of books manufactured, selling little more than 200 copies, paid for by the families, spouses, and friends of the author.

Its not a surprise for the collector of rare editions to find copies of books which are hand numbered in the colophon and signed, "To my friend, Bob."

The vanity press became so distained in the publsihing field, that often it was considered social suicide to self publish a book, and was always considered disasterous in terms of "return on investment". Often, the book would cost more to produce than was made on sales. Vanity presses promised to make as many copies of a book, as fancy as you liked, for as much money as you could afford to dump into such as wasteful project. The more money you wasted, the better.

As technology grew, printing became much easier. Xerography made book publishing a rather simple process, and offset printing from photo engraved plates became standard. Many newspapers today are still printed using this method. Eventually, we got smart, and were able to begin producing books in smaller "on demand" runs with a photo-copier. These machines were still clunky and expensive, but many decent books were produced using them. Again, cost was a factor.

Again, with the advent of computers, the ability to type, edit, and manufacture a book became much easier for the author to do. Saving a copy to disk and going back to fix problems is much easier, and printing from home makes sending off those -once expensive- manuscripts to publishers so much easier.

I still remember the first author I met with a Tandy computer (with a monochrome monitor and dot matrix printer, the kind with the paper attatched by a perforated edge and holes on the sides to keep it in line in the printer) who was able to inexpensively produce his first book himself. It took eight hours to print off the manuscript. Yes, this was before Microsoft Word and the laser-jet.

In the end, photo-copies of this book were bound up by the local printing house and sold to local stores for a ridiculous sum, but he made some money, and the self published writer became something of a local celebrity. It was even cooler if he used a neat font.

How I got started in publishing

It was the summer of 2003. My girlfriend and I decided to get married after a year of high school upgrading, and as we were making wedding preparations, I realized, "Hey, waitaminit! What do I have to offer this girl?" I had no money, no job prospects, no career, I was enrolling to start College in the fall, and was living off of my summer job and what remained of my student loans.

That we had no money was clear as day - enough to get by on, but not enough to start a big business. After considering what it was I enjoyed doing, I realized that I could easily start an Ebay business, selling chapbooks of essays and articles. It was a neat idea, so I took my last $5 bill and went and bought a ream of paper at the office supply store, and set up an Ebay account.

We got married on July 23, and went on a 2 week camping trip with my kids in Fort St. John. While we were away, our little books sold 20 copies at $5.00 each, netting us over $80 in profits. From a minimal investment, I knew we had something.

Over the following year, we increased sales to $300/month, expanded our line to 14 books, and learned how to get softcover books printed at a really decent price. At the end of our first year, we had made a million mistakes, sold hundreds of books, and were starting to expand our line to hardcovers.

Our book bindery skills were increasing, as were our resources.

We started manufacturing our own books out of our little one bedroom basement suite apartment, selling on Ebay and to local stores. We had enough to pay our rent, but not enough to say that we were terribly successful as publishers.

Local book binderies were of little help, as the theme seemed to be "We are not going to train our competition."

Eventually, we expanded our business into small edition press runs of hardcover books. Looking back, these things were ugly as heck, but we learned what to do and what not to do. We had expanded our business to owning a couple of decent printers, our product was looking spectacular (after some trial and error, learning how to print and bind our own covers. We were sellign about $1000 in softcover books online by this time, at $15 for a softcover book. The chapbooks had been left behind, as people were not as interested in them (I have a friend who took over this line, and makes a couple hundred extra a month from it).

Our bindery grew. We started binding in leather, and established more suppliers and contacts in the industry. We bound our first university dissertation during the summer of 2006, and our book bindery was in full swing. We got a Yellow Pages ad, a seperate phone, and a were binding hardcover journals for sale at local book stores and gift shops. People began seeking us out, and our custom bindery operation grew in earnest.

2007 brought its share of heartaches and expansions. We bought a retail location in Downtown Calgary, expanded our sales to corporate groups, including the Calgary Stampede, and many more retailers. Every expansion was more exciting than the ones previous.

2008, tragedy struck with a divorce from my wife, but the bindery continued to grow. Through the year we purchased equipment from several failign businesses, thus expanding our abilities, and in October, we purchased the Calgary Book Bindery, an 83 year old company, and a piece of Calgary's history. The equipment we sought for so long was finally in our office.

In 2008, our little book publishing houses were combined into a single publishing house, called ALEPHA PUBLISHING. We were approached by a young university graduate who had stumbled upon our books in the University bookstore, and wanted to create a new publishing concept. Its been a year in the development, and we are ready to release our first series, with a back list of over 200 titles.

Its been pretty exciting. Now, on to the work of doing more, having more, and being more.

If you have any questions, I'd be more than happy to try to answer them for you.

Do a favor and check out some of our advertising sponsors. They have some great material for researching the industry, and also some very good services that may help you on your way. Go ahead, it doesn't cost you a dime.

How do I get published?

Q: I've written a book and am looking to have it published. What do I need to do?

A: As a publisher, I've heard this question hundreds of times. My favorite by far is, "Its so great, its going to sell a million copies. You've gotta help me,I'm going to make you a millionaire!"

As an artist, my first thought is "Wow, great accomplishment, I'm so proud of you!"

As a businessman, my first thought is, "Is it good enough to read?"

If its a good read, then I'm interested in publishing it. If the ideas are sound, if the writing flows, if the story grabs me, then I'm interested. If its nonsense, poorly written, or doesn't really have what it takes to keep me interested after a brief 2 minute scan of the pages, then I'm sorry, I'm not going to risk investing my money into a project.

Artists have to be honest with themselves. Writing is a business, it is a real career with skills that can be learned and taught. I do believe that everyone with a pen should be writing, but not necessarily for a profit. Some people should be sharing their stories, journaling, writing letters to their friends and family, keeping in touch.

Many publishers won't even look at an unsolicited manuscript. Most will check out a brief synopsis, a paragraph covering the concept and storyline. One of the biggest mistakes a writer makes is the shotgun approach to getting published, sending their book off to 100 publishers, in hopes that one will take the chance on them. Remember that people are investing real money into a publishing project, unless they see value, they won't put money into it. Its as simple as that. Instead, the writer should make contact with a publishing agent.

What is an agent? They act on your behalf with the publishing houses, for a percentage of your profit. In short, they are your advocate, they approach the right people in the right way, so that you have a much better chance of getting your book produced.

Agents are expensive, and usually they are not your coach.I know many that offer editing services and ghost writing services as a part of their approach to creating sellable product. They WILL critique your work, and suggest changes. Listen to them, they are trying to help you make a sellable product, and in my opinion, if they say its drivel, it usually is.

I know a local agent that also owns a small press publishing house, because there are a ton of people who can't get published under a normal publishing house, but can benefit from purchasing a small press run of their own books. That leads us into self publishing, which I will discuss later.

So, in short, there are two approaches to getting published:

1) send a synopsis to see if they're interested in reading more,
2) contact an agent, and listen to their advice.

I'm very sure that I will write more on this subject as I go along. I hope you enjoyed this, and do a favor and invite your friends to check out this blog. If any of the ads ont his page interest you, please check them out too. They are there for your perusal. Its my opinion that intelligence (in the sense of gathering information) is a great way to understand the industry.

A Cautionary Tale

I awoke, as we all must wake in the morning light when the time is come upon us to open our eyes and greet the sun with its brilliant intensity upon the darkness of our sleep.

I was a child, full with the dew of sleep upon my lids, the hunger for mothers milk upon my cries, my mother's breast awaiting my suckling lips. There is little more that I remember of this era of my life, so strange and unrelated it seems to the years that follow.

My father spoke of how much my mother loved and adored me when I was a child, barely old enough to think clearly beyond my body's basic needs. Quench my thirst, feed my stomach, change my diaper, talk to me in that cooing voice filled with a new mother's sentimentality.

If I did not know better now, after all of these years of tribulation, I would think that this child might have a chance to live a normal life, a life of peace, pleasure, and joy. But instead, God awoke in his family a wrath unfitting to digest. This little child's family would be torn apart under the gaze of green jealousy and red rapture, blackened with a lifetime of hate and fear.

There were the stories I grew up with, the tales of lust and debauchery which I scarcely understood, and yet longed to know more about. Madness would drive me to scratch through the surface of a family's broken heart and seek deeper into the red blood which pulsed beneath its gaudy surface. Soaked with sweat, I would be awakened from a terrible nightmare, only to discover that I had only awakened to a more dreadful reality.

What some children take for granted I never knew. I reached for it in my own children, only to let them down with the knowledge I was missing.

Momentum

Repeating the results of past successes
Is like turning the crank on a bicycle
At first it may seem difficult to get started
But once you are going,
Momentum makes it easier
The resistance seems less difficult
To overcome.

The choice with every rotation
With every push
Is to keep pushing
To keep rhythm
In your strokes
Which makes keeping your balance
easier.

But what strokes matter?
What strokes are the ones
With the biggest payout?

Make your strokes worth more
Give them more value
Push for bigger gains
Higher value
More fun
Excitement

Profit in everything
Not just money

Profit in friends
Profit in good times
Profit in good deeds
Profit in smiles
Profit in happiness
Profit in little successes
------The money WILL come.
Building momentum takes time.
Building momentum takes practice.
Building momentum takes patience.
Keep your eye on the goal.
Keep your eye on the goal.
Keep your eye on the goal,
And you will always gain it.

Why you will never know...

Yes, its true,
You will never know.
Not because I don't want you to know
But because you would never understand.
The way I feel about us
Has little to do with how you feel about me.
It has to do with
All of the things that
Make us who we are
And that is why I love you.
You have no idea
The lengths I would go
To show you how much
I love you
But I will never tell you
In a way that you would accept.
I would give everything
Just to be with you
Everything
Except the truth
I will never tell you
Because you will never know.
I would let you go
So that you will come back
I will let you be with others
If that is what would make you happy
That I would marry you is no question
Because in my mind we are already married
In a way more real than vows

In a way more real than a ring
In a way more real than sharing your bed
In a way more real than sharing a home
It is love, pure, satisfying, committed,
It is a love I will never admit to
Because we have already discussed this
You do not understand
And I accept that.
Its okay.

You will never know,
Because I will not tell you.
You are not ready for it.
Perhaps in another lifetime
Perhaps in this one.
I wait for you
To come to me.
That is the way it is,
That is the way it should be.

Socialism, Corporatism, and Monopolism

Socialism = begging for a handout, being made to feel terrible when you get it, and waiting forever to receive it. Socialism looks great on the books, but look at how its played out in reality, and watch the horror on anyone's face who's had to live with it.

I am an anti-corporatist, anti-socialist capitalist. I believe in freedom, and the reality is that if you offer a service of value to other members of your community, they will pay you what they think it is worth, or they will find someone else who will give it to them for what they can afford, or they will do without.

Bankruptcy is a crime.
Corporatism is a crime.
Monopolism is a crime.

The crashing economy is a result of all of these crimes. As a result, those slaves to the almighty "security" have to learn to fend for themselves.

Corporatism breeds incompetence. Socialism breeds "The least amount of effort for the most amount of security". Both are cons, and you can never con an honest person.

How Robert is NOT being a Drama Queen...

A disagreement does not extend to insults. An argument in a literary sense is a series of statements based on supporting a thesis. Where these statements may be countered and rebutted with supporting evidence, sometimes the evidence must be proven false or disregarded as out of context. There is no need to undermine a person's self worth in the process.

Thusly, if you cannot argue rationally and with integrity, then I agree that it may be a wise move to end the relationship. But as to abandonment, the only person here being attacked is me. To flee an attack in order to maintain my calm and to keep from angry outbursts is in no way "abandoning", it is keeping me from falling into old habits.

Believe me, me walking away at a time like this is VERY good for both of us. You have not experienced an angry Robert, and my walking away prevents you from experiencing such behavior.

I appreciate your concern, which I'm sure underlies your opinion, but your concern does not make that opinion true.

NOTES:

From therapy I've learned that Anger is not a primary emotion in response to a situation, it is a secondary emotion in response to our primary emotions of fear, frustration, confusion, etc. Anger is a product of other emotions, and is an action taken in response to them. Once we realize this, we are able to take other actions instead.

In this particular case, my action was to walk away to get some sleep, and then to consider things when I am more capable - id est, in the morning when I've gotten some rest. Tell you the truth, I am still thinking things over, and have not come to a solid conclusion yet.

I know what things I want in my life, I know what things I don't want in my life. I guess I have to consider which of these is more important. I don't want drama, insults, and unhealthy arguing. I do want a calm environment, rational communication, and a reasonable partner. One cannot exist where the other does. I will walk if it continues. I will not return if it is not resolved.

Deception

You wrote to me the other day that, "I am only trying to see my daughter to poke at you and not really because my fatherly instincts are so developed" (non-verbatim).

So tell me, why would I have any need at all to "poke at you"? You have done enough to lose respect in my eyes this past year as both a parent and as a reasonable human being. I avoid communication with you as much as humanly possible, including attempting to minimize contact with you when you drop off or pick up our daughter.

There have been three instances since we split up where you refused access to our daughter for over a month at a time. There are hundreds of instances this past year (yes, literally) where you would not answer your cell phone or text messages to allow me to talk with her.

We had arranged for me to see her every weekend, and then you consistently made plans with your friends to watch her instead. You refused to allow her to see her brother and sister when I had them on three occasions.

Your accusations do not only extend to me, but also to my son. You claimed that you did not want him to see her for a whole weekend because he could not be trusted, citing that "a single parent is not watchful enough".

This summer, you attempted to involve me in your drama involving a person at Cafe Beano who had an altercation with your boyfriend, by telling me and other people that he knew that your boyfriend had "police reports" that included a list of charges including rape, and that if I didn't stop hanging around this person, that you'd not allow me to see her again at all. You then trumped up some accusation against him the same week of the altercation that he threatened your life at the same coffee shop, in front of a bunch of witnesses who claim that you were no where near him at the time. Finally, you tried to convince me that he "admitted his guilt" to the police, knowing full well that had he done so he'd be charged with uttering threats and immediately put in jail because of his probation order. Why would anyone go to such lengths to manipulate and control me? Oh, yeah, he got into a fist fight with your boyfriend. You also claimed to me that this happened in front of our daughter, when in fact neither of you were there

Your best friend when we split up got on the wrong side of your boyfriend as well. I seem to recall that he was going to run over a dog in the middle of the road, and she yelled at him to stop, saying something like, "How would you like someone to run over your children?" He of course, took this as an insult, or a threat (way overboard), screamed and yelled at her, kicked her out of the car before it stopped moving, and then told you that she threatened his kids. You, of course, took his side, saying that you didn't want to be caught in the middle of it. The following week, he harassed her with threatening text messages, claiming that he wasn't "her bitch" and threatened her life more than once - all so that she would return a flash drive with her pictures on it. Of course, you believed his story and ditched your best friend, even after she forwarded the text messages to you.

Now, again, your boyfriend has contacted me (after eight months of silence following me telling him never to contact me again, that he was not welcome to talk with me or my

73

children) with threatening text messages and Facebook stalking. (yes, that's how I know that you are going to get this message).

The first series of messages implied that I was telling my daughter stories about his being a murderer. The second was that I had threatened his life. The first message was send after I texted you to say that I wouldn't be able to pick her up because I was too ill. The second came at 12AM the next Sunday. One week apart, both after I was to see my daughter. Your next message was that I had somehow told the police an untruth when I had called them on him. I gave the officer the messages exactly as I had received them. Yet again, the only person you will believe in this case is your boyfriend.

Frankly, I can't blame you, he's the guy that pays for the roof over your head and the Mercades you drive. Why would you want to risk losing all of that hard earned money he spends on you?

If he texts me again, I will call the police again. It will continue until he gets the point that these games are not welcome.

As to spending time with my daughter, I expect you to follow the arrangement we'd previously agreed upon, or that we arrange for mediation so that we can put something in writing.

Last Words

To the people I love, remember that I am with you, always. I may not have been the greatest person you knew, but my love was true, if not expressed in the fullest.

Life is tough, I know. The hand does not always act with the best of intentions, but know that I tried to do my best - it wasn't always enough, but my heart was on a path to purity, if purity was not yet achieved.

I know that honesty was not always my strongest suit, but my lies were often to keep from hurting you, to protect you from the truth. I'm sorry if I ever lied for any other reason. I'm sure it happened often enough, and I regret any straying words.

I have not always been the most respectable person, in fact, there are a great many things I regret in my life. I have hurt many people, most of them people who were close to my heart, people who loved me. I am sorry, and hope that in time you will find it acceptable to forgive me.

To my children, I am sorry that I was not a very good father. I did not know what that meant until it was much too late, and I had damaged your world too much to fix. I love you, and am sorry that I could not provide for you the lives that you deserved, with the constant love and stability I wanted to give you.

To my wives and girlfriends, I love you all. I know that I was a bugger, a brat, and a bitch at times. You did not deserve the hardness of my words or the harsh actions I may have had at times. No matter how hard I tried to change, it was an upward battle. I do hope you know that you have inspired me to be a better person, if only because you helped teach me the hardest lessons.

Mom, I know we have not had the best of relationships. You hurt me so much that I never really healed from it. I felt abandoned the better part of my life, and unfortunately, passed that terror on to my own children. It is a cruel world, and in our family, cruelty began at home. I'm sorry for anything mean I ever did or said to hurt you. I'm sorry that I wasn't the son you wanted me to be. I'm sorry that I hated you for so long for leaving me, for allowing us kdis to be abused by your boyfriends. I would like to think it made us stronger, but the emotional damage was simply not worth it.

Dad, the more I've gotten to know you, the more I appreciate and love you. I wish I was a better son to you, and am sorry for the tears I brought you. You are a good man, even when you were too hard on me. I regret that I never really lived up to your standards, and I'm sorry if I never made you very proud of me. I was trying to live up to standards of my own making, and I know I failed dreadfully a these tasks I gave myself. I hate to think that I didn't live up to your standards. I know it hurt you when I left, and I know you were hurt that I didn't make it to your wedding. I love you, and hope that the memories you remember are the better ones.

To my friends, please know that I love you. You were all supportive, loving, giving, and filled me with hope and wonder. I don't know how to tell you how you've helped me to be a better person. In all cases, I've learned from you, and in spite of my own foolishness, I know that you loved me enough to keep pushing me forwards, cheering me on from the sidelines, coaching me, mentoring me, helping me, entertaining me, and above all, loving me. If I ever hurt you, please forgive me. I know I am nto the easiest person to love, but you did. To me, that is an accomplishment.

Should I die tomorrow, know that all of this is true.

There is nowhere to put the things I have amassed in this lifetime. They are treasures to me, but likely garbage to anyone else. Please, sell my belongings, give my clothing to charity, auction my library to pay for my debts, and if anything remains, put it in trust for my children. Currently, it isn't much, but I do hope that they can get something out of my life.

Please, burn my body and spread the ashes to the sky from the top of a building or a mountain.

Its Been Awhile

Its been awhile
Since I've written
About Love.

But Love Sings
Still in the heavens
And on the Earth.

Even now
As the sky bleeds
Bitter tears.

We held on
In spite of the sky
Collapsing

You piece me
Together when
All is lost.

Love is
Everlasting,
My Goddess.

Even now,
Its been awhile
In darkness

The sun

Rises over the
Horizon

The halo
Touches the
Morning.

The Green Man

Victor Grobel was a man of many words and few talents. He hob-nobbled with the victims of circumstance, telling a stray joke here, a short blather there, rarely discussing anything of any importance with anyone of any significance. Victor was a man who, in spite of this appearance, knew how to tell one end of a chicken from another, but not necessarily what kind of chicken to which he was speaking to.

Victor was a hard man to follow, wandering from this end of the city to another, never seeming to get much done, but always seeming to do something. No one really knew what Victor's job was, but he was, in fact, quite proud of his post as Bridge and Tunnel Inspector for the State. In reality, his position also extended to the Sewers and Manholes of the city, and as long as he was able to write a decent report at the end of the day, he was given leave to wander as he might, inspecting as he inspected, and chatting joyously to whomever might listen.

Victor could tell a story like no other, spreading a yarn from one end of the line to another as fast as the ear could hear. So extensive was this man of words, that one day he happened upon his ability to put it all into writing. The idea staggered him, as old Mrs. Sinclair from the Pickle Road Deli suggested that he try to capture his tongue in the form of ink on a scrap of paper. His stories were ones of mischief and vigorous debauchery, lining up his ridiculous gossips like a series of bottles ready to be knocked down by a garrulous pistol. He was not a vicious man, in fact, his stories were rarely true, and in fact, from one day to the next he'd draw upon a gathering of satires, so widely distributed across the city that, like a rumor in the telling, would expand and contract from one block to another, differing in both detail and exaggeration as he traveled up and down the city streets. He'd pull from one conversation a random name, a figure here, a detail there, expressions shifting like desert sands upon a rocky wasteland of words and phrases.

Uninvited

So, I wax heavily on the idiocy's I've produced in my depression.

I have been uninvited to an event.

Apparently, I was not a good enough friend to be told by the people I've offended, and am rather pleased to note that, were the same situation presented to me, I would have been (and indeed, have been) a decent enough person to have let them know in person, as an aside, or in an Email.

As I generally know the sources of such contempt, I can point out to them that for all their friendship and kindness I've been shown in their past relationships with me, it is much easier to toss a friend away than to face them with your concerns, no matter how significant.

Thanks for your support, love, trust and understanding.

In the same shoes, for the most of you, I have given the shirt off of my back, have held you in the deepest parts of your own sadness and emotional instability, and have been there whenever called upon. Until taken advantage of, in the case of some of my "friends".

I will be the first to admit that the charges laid against me are quite true - I am a bit of a shit when drunk lately, and my behavior towards a certain few (very few, I might add) women have been based as much on their having taken advantage of a situation as much as it was my having taken advantage of it. Call me a scapegoat, and I will be happy to take the entire blame, if it makes you feel better about yourself in the morning.

As I've recently written, "Friends become strangers. Love is not real because it can be betrayed." Even when hurt and humiliated, I still count you amongst my friends. No one is removed from my facebook, no one's numbers have been taken off of my phone. I will still call you as if this were merely another day. But since so many were not willing to come to me with the same trust I have given them, I can only say that I'm better off not knowing you.

So, shame on me for expressing my pain.
Shame on you for not being honest.

Only To Dream

I drempt of you last night.
That I held you again
Close to me
Loving me
Promising the world to me
Something I wished for
So deeply and so long.

I drempt of you last night,
And realized
That I still love you
And it hurt me to realize
That it was only a dream
When I did wake up
You were gone.

I asked you, "What are you doing?"
When you held my hand
And pulled me close.
You answered,
"Don't you still believe in magick?"
And I realized
That even in my dreams
You conquer me,
Pull me down
To a world I know nothing about.

My faith is lost.
If it were only for that

I would have nothing more.

I have witnessed miracles,
Strange events and tests of will,
I have met God, firsthand
I have seen candles light themselves
And witnessed spontaneous manifestations

And yet...

I do not believe anymore.
Through the lens of a broken heart
I cannot see the world as magickal.
In a world of broken dreams
I have loved and lost
And realized that
Impermanence is everything.
Life is but a dream,
And I am no longer in control.

I loved you once,
Perhaps that is enough,
For to love once is to
Love forever.

I cannot believe in magick
Because it could not heal me
From losing you.

So I ask myself,
Do you still dream of me,
Wishing for me again,
In the realms of your sleep?
Do you ever ask yourself,
Do you ever wonder,
Do you ever cling to your pillow

Begging to sleep again
So that you can
Experience magick again?

Perhaps I am asking too much of the world
To wish for our lives to once again
Cross paths and unite us as once we had,
Our universes intertwined,
With new lessons learned
And a world of change before us,
The one thing unchanging.

But in that dream,
You are only a part of me,
A piece of my mind,
Which shows you how deeply
You have affected me,
To have become a part of me,
A voice in my head,
A face in my dreams,
A longing in my heart -
As real as the tears
Staining my face.

Could I believe in magick again?
I don't know.
It is my religion,
And I have lost faith,
The dark night of the soul
Pulling me away from
That which I knew was real.

I think back and remember
The miracles we shared -
The glowing crystal
The child conceived

The homes we manifested
The dollar bills from heaven
The grimoire of our lives
Written moment by moment.

I thank the universe for you,
To have been with you once,
And would not have changed that
For anything.
For anything...
But to be with you again.

Saw You Today

I saw you today
And my heart turned cold
Steel bars surrounding me
Love turns to pain
So quickly it seems.

All I hear from you are lies
All I see in you is pain
All you ever fed me was poison.
All you ever speak of is hate.

Then you have the nerve to ask me
Whats wrong with me,
When you've lied, cheated, and stolen
All that mattered to me.

Now you threaten to leave me penniless
And yet you say you don't hate me
And you say you don't love me
You only want to be done with me

You brought nothing to the table
You brought nothing to the bed
You destroyed my children's lives,
You've destroyed my faith in love.

You ask me whats wrong with me?
Fuck you. You are whats wrong with me.
I saw you today, and you reminded me
Of everything thats wrong in the world.

DOM SLK - Gangsta Mafioso (12.34)

We rode through the streets
Packing heat
Just a little pistol
Carrying a little crystal
Walk into the club'an
Hanging out with the cubans
Shaking hands with columbians
Moving with urban legends
We were seeking admiration
The girls offering libations
The boys talking trash
Behind our backs
Does it matter? No
Its only a little slander,
Makes them look worse
Words put you in a hearse
If it were up to me
We'd be drug runnin,
Making more more money
Than working
Someone said
'never heard of ya'
Thats good
Keeping low
Stead of murderin'
Keep hustlin'
Bustlin,
Bust a line
Instead of capping ya

Keeping clean
Case they testing ya
The rest of ya
Graspin at favors
Calling up the neighbors
In case they bustin ya
Got a crush on ya
Call the cops on ya
Keep the peace
On the streets
Don't attract attention
Just don't mention
What you do for a livin,
Not lookin' for trouble
Cause troubles gone a find ya
Back window blows out on ya
Some bastard comes to slaughter ya
Put a draw on ya,
Cause freedom has a price
Sell a little bit of ice
Dealing with the lowest
Eyes become the coldest
Pull the trigger
Nothin' happens
One more angel watch'n over
A gangster mafioso
I'm a king not a soldier
Get another year older
Start learning what I came for
Thats the game, tho
Back in the day, brother
Ain't the same, cousin

DOM SLK - Into You (4:40)

Girl, you've got my head turning
With all things you've been saying,
You think I'm only playing,
I apologize if I've got you thinking

You say that you want to be just friends,
But girl, thats the beginning of the end,
We play together, but thats just pretend,
I told you once, but I'll tell you again

Sorry, but I'm not that into you.
You think you're hot shit
Cause you've got all these boys after you,

I think its funny, I'm not that into you
So you say that's it,
There's nothing more I want to say to you.

You tell me that I'm like your family,
You tell your friends that you don't like me,
I try to show you, but you don't want to see
You won't hear what you won't believe,

There was a time that I thought you might,
A good friendship was what we felt was right,
But then you had to go and spell it out that night,
I'm telling you that I don't give up without a fight.

Sorry, but I'm not that into you.

You think you're hot shit
Cause you've got all these boys after you,

I think its funny, I'm not that into you
So you say that's it,
There's nothing more I want to say to you.

DOM SLK - Second Rap Title (1:25)

I learned at a young age to take care of myself,
No love for me,
no family,
Left my heart back there on the shelf.

I've had to build a sense of certainty
That I'd be taken care of,
When things got tough,
I'd still try to keep my integrity.

If it wasn't for your parents' wealth,
You'd have nothing,
You've lost something,
You've never learned to take care of yourself.

So instead you sell your body to the highest bidder,
Nothing but looks and glamor,
Nothing but words and slander,
You're nothing but a shallow quitter.

You don't care for anyone but yourself,
Never learned to love,
Empty kisses and hugs,
Nothing but words in an empty mouth.

I've met crack whores with more respect than you,
Always coming unglued
When your dreams don't come true,
Skipping out on your kids when they don't suit you.

If there's one thing I've learned taking care of my own,
Is nothing lasts forever,
No Hell, no Heaven,
You took my life, my kids, my world, my home.

But there's one thing I know, deep down,
Is that I will always be loved,
If not taken care of,
And that I will always stay true to my vows.

The only kind of thing that remains true
Love changes,
Friends become strangers,
Eventually I will heal, and rise above you.

Notes:

Catherine: Were is this coming from? Are you writing this for a friend or for yourself? This is pretty deep and makes me wonder what u think life has done to you and to let u know that I love you and am here now. Sorry I wasn't in the past.

Robert: Cat, I've been writing a rap album to help me heal from the past shit and abuse I've taken and dished out. I didn't deserve such a shit filled life, but its what I've got. I should be glad its not worse.

People look up to me to be a role model, a mentor, a confidant, and a all around good decent kind of guy. They see that I've come through a lot ofcrap, and clawed my way up tooth and nail. Little do they know that I've come from a world of hurt, and they don't see it on the surface.

N. is the only person I've met thus far that can read my face and mannerisms so well that she knows when I'm about to cry hours before it happens.

My world is one of abandonment. My lessons are hard learned. People are shits. They created a monster, and its all I can do to keep alive day to day.

I never thought I'd write a rap album, but its helping, at least its keeping me from killing the bastard that ruined my life.

100,000 words (Or at least, the first 4500)

This is a race to 100,000 words. At about 1,000 words per page, its near 100 pages of writing. I've done that before - in face, a small-ish article for a magazine is about 1,200 words. A letter to a friend is about 750. The average government form is 200. I'll admit, I'd rather do the former two than the latter one, but I likely write a million words a year. And that is my goal for 2009, my 33rd year, 1 Million words. Ten novels. Ten one hundred page books. Its a huge commitment in time and energy, but I'm up to the challenge. (103 words already, and I haven't even begun).

So, I started my 33rd year with a pout and a frown. The day before my birthday I slept on the couch at my store, avoiding my unhappy roommates, and the night before that alone, drinking far too much brandy and laying on the floor for hours to try and straighten out the kink in my back.

I woke this morning with the best of intentions, quick coffee, then off for breakfast at the local greasy spoon. I decided to patch things up with my roommate and invite her out for brekkie, but to no avail. She's not a morning person, and yelled at me, "I'll meet you at the store. I don't like being rushed." No "Happy Birthday". No hug. No love. Go back to sleep, hon. Don't do me any favors. I guess thats what I get for sleeping with my roommates - no rent, no love, just the occasional (hard earned) cuddle and no food in the cupboard.

Okay, so I guess that's not the best start to a birthday or to a novel, but I'm sure it gets better at the end. I'm going to take a quick break now for a cigarette and to avoid talking to my little sister, who thinks that instant messaging is the way to redevelop an already estranged relationship. I guess she was the second happy birthday greeting I got today, the first being a girl I was texting on my phone last night. She got in late from a date, and got the text I sent her inviting her out for dinner after work. Sadly, she declined, but offered a coffee next week instead. I guess that's something, but not really what I had in mind for my birthday evening.

...
...
...

Now, you might notice a lot of typos...I'm not fixing them as I go along. This challenge is to get to 100,000 words in a month, so there's a lot of time for my editor to fix the problems. I'm not going to concern myself with them. Grind out the words, don't' worry about the content. IT can be fixed later. . I'm shooting for 1 Million in a year. I mean, all things considered, that's a pretty tough goal to meet, especially without a plot or anything really read-worthy. I suppose I could have spent a couple of hours writing a decent outline - take up ten pages or so developing my characters, draw out my sub-plots, think about some fashionably hip names for my characters, like Kiesha or Medula, but I think I'll stick to a relatively real taste of my less than ordinary life. OR is that more than extraordinary? Depends on who you talk to. I;'ve a lot of friends who are convinced that my melancholy is unreasonable, even when you consider the divorce that's been looming on the horizon of my life this past six months.

Okay, so divorce...not much to say about that. Fairy tale romance goes to shit when wife starts fucking her friend she met at the coffee shop. Throw in a dash of attempted suicide, some long hours in counseling with my therapist, and the kids being abandoned at the school by their step mother one beautiful Thursday afternoon so that she can go fuck him across town, and you've pretty much got that story in a nut-sack. Are the kids hurt? yes. Is the husband hurt? yes. Does she care? No, of course not. Its a fairy tale romance, she is, of course, the princess, who was saved from the tower of her boredom by the nerdy nobody, only for her to be taken in by the Dragon later on in the romance. She's now living it up in a life of illusion, the Dragon spending ludicrous amounts of treasure on her to make her feel like she's something special, all the while holding his gifts above her head any time she decides to leave him - "go ahead then, leave. Just pay me the money you owe me first." Nerdy Nobody's daughter, the ballerina fairy princess, calls this monster "Daddy Dragon", who attempts to poison her against her father, by telling her that it was HE who left, not the overly beautiful, but not too loyal princess. The dragon begins to dangle another carrot of control before he droopy mesmerized eyes of the princess, by telling her that she too can have riches like his. He puts her to work as his assistant, and the cords tighten around her wrists, magickal chains of control, invisible to the mortal eye, but noticed only by the Nerdy Nobody, who, as it turns out has been practicing magic his whole life, under the tutelage of some of the world's greatest masters (because, you see, Nerdy Nobody is a bookbinder and bookstore owner...he is a nerd, after all...), but alas, non of them are living, only speaking to him from the echo in their books. He knows them intimately, the details of their careers, the methods to their madness, the devices they used in summoning up the spirits. But, his heart is broken, and he cannot cast magick at her. The dragon has his revenge - the Nerdy Nobody cannot cast. The princess is under his spell, and the little fairy princess is being consumed by the Dragon's paranoia and hatred. The nerdy nobody takes to drinking brandy and scotch in the aloneness of his tiny apartment, his roommates adding a modicum of entertainment in the form of worldly dramas to his life, and the Dragon wins, because he has convinced the Princess that it was an abusive relationship to begin with, otherwise she wouldn't have been compelled to leave him, cheat on him, or abandon her children for him...no worries, love. We all know that the greatest enemy is within, and until you can let go of the need to justify your trashy behavior, you will remain under his spell...no one, not even the Nerdy Nobody...especially not the nerdy nobody, can save her. She is trapped in her own delusion, and no one lives happily ever after.

Hey, I never said this story had a happy ending. Only that it was a Fairy tale romance. Problem with fairy tales, is that after the "happily ever after part", the shit hits the fan, but we don't want to break all the little boys and girls' hearts with reality, now, do we?

...
...
...

So, I've decided on a title for this little ditty: "A Life Worth Living". Not that catchy, but neither is the tune. Its a dirge, if you will, recounting the days of shame and wrath that the heart of a good man endures. Its the tale of Lot, a man who's had the world stripped from him. Unfortunately, its also the story of a man who's lost his faith, and no gods capable of giving it back.

I've been seeking the meaning to all of this. Therein lies the rub, that there is no meaning except as we decide to give it.

Always searching for the silver lining, and not finding much that its certain or salvageable.

I could call it, "Life, and How to Live It", but I'm a novice at this whole living thing. Funny thing for a bookstore owner to say, but I sell hundreds of books on this very subject, and well read in the philosophies of life, and still have no idea what the hell I'm on about.

The trouble with finding a title is that you typecast the whole idea right from the start. This book is more a practice in free writing than an actual novel, but I suppose the story itself will come out by the end.

I'm full of sarcastic witticisms today, most of them heartfelt jargon of a bygone era - call me a romantic. Call me an anachronism. I used to think of myself as a renaissance man, but got muscled out by the guys with better clothes and more money than I have. When asked for my resume, I challenged, "I paint, I write, I bind beautiful books, I am a jeweler, and a sculptor, I have a massive collection of rare and antique books (that I read), and enjoy sharing what I have learned with others. I study and practice philosophy and magic. I enjoy great wines and can understand the subtleties in a single malt scotch. I tend to be literary in that way - always seeking the right words for the wrong circumstances. I've overcome many of my addictions, and have drowned in the sea of vice. I have been learning to conquer myself, and fear mainly that the art of subtlety may be lost amongst the masses. I enjoy the study of humanity without taking part in it. I am a god amongst mortals, and a mortal amongst gods." They rejected my application on the grounds of my immorality.

I am reminded of a story by my friend Elliott. I'll paraphrase:

On the day that mankind awakened to the realization that religion was an invention, Hades went to Sisyphus and said, "That's it, you're off the hook." Sisyphus ignored him and continued to roll the boulder up the hill, shouldering his burden as if he had not heard him, for indeed, he had not.

After a brief conversation with a goddess I know and adore, I read her cards, and up came the Hermit. We are seeking something that is within us, but we are searching for it outside of ourselves. We thirst, but cannot drink enough to sate it. We eat, but the food turns to dust on our lips. We make love, but the desire never abates. We yearn for something, but cannot find anything to fill the emptiness. Our hearts are hardened against hearing the words we know contain the key to ending our search, and yet, we search because we know not what else to do. The glass is neither half empty nor half full, it is broken, and we are attempting to sweep up the pieces without further cutting ourselves on the shards.

...

...

...

Life just isn't that literary. Sure, there are brief moments of foreshadowing, interesting plot twists where it turns out that the good guy is in fact an asshole and learns to blame himself for what's gone wrong in his little adventure, but all in all, life is really pretty boring and not very noteworthy. Is it really that interesting to learn that the protagonist is really his own antagonist?

Happy Birthday, Bobby. You're life is shit. Make something great of it.

My doctor said, "Suicide attempts are done for attention. Whose attention are you trying to get?" You weren't there, dude. The tattoos cover the scars. I had learned that I was the antagonist in another person's story. I didn't want to be that. Better a lunatic on the fringe than the character that her audience might despise. (In one's life story, it is the author who also happens to be the audience...no one else really bothers to read it). She forced the door open and took the blade away. I couldn't see very well for the tears. She curled my head in her lap and told me I had a lot to live for. Then she slept with someone else that night. "Why would you do that to your children?" she asked. A few months later she would abandon them at school. Are these little ironies what makes life interesting? Catcher in the Rye would have us believe that people are shits. We're all guilty of hypocrisy. We're all shits. But to keep ourselves from believing it, we justify everything and pretend like we're the good guys. We're all a bunch of cowards, hiding from the grim realities of the truth. WE suck.

...
...
...

Chapter Two - A Letter

K.

Are you putting me on notice, or pulling the reins on yourself?

Last I checked, I was under the impression that we were friends. Have I given you the impression that I was after something more?

In my world, a friendship can often turn into much more, and that love itself is undifferentiated - there is no limit to what it can be, or with whom. Generally speaking, I would rather a long term friendship with someone I loved than a short term romance. Romance dies, friendship remains, even after the romance has gone. There are three kinds of love, Eros, Philia, and Agape.

Eros, sexual love (or romantic love), is what people relate to the idea of "Falling in Love". It is the kind of love that the common, earthy person looks for. Sexual attraction, chemistry, obsession. This is what people think "True Love" is. But, it never lasts. It is not meant to last. This is often called by many "puppy love" or "Lust". Deep attachment to another, jealousy, ownership, and passion are associated with this kind of love.

Philia is brotherly love, the love between friends and family. It is the most common, and the most long lasting. This kind of relationship is based on the caring of another individual, the desire to see them succeed in life, and to help them to do so. Philia can easily be transformed into either of the other two loves by simple expression, pacing the relationship into a different form. But regardless of the form it takes, Philia will always remain.

Finally, there is Agape, deep, unconditional love. This is the kind of love that a person must first find for themselves before they can realize it in others. Agape is the truest love there is, and comes from the wish for one's fellow person to be happy. Unconditional love can be felt for a mate, just as much as it can be felt for a friend, lover, or stranger. It is often best expressed in the Hindu term, "Namaste", meaning, "The divine in me recognizes the divine in you."

Generally speaking, the three kinds cannot be confused with each other on a subtle, physical level. A priest often feels Agape for his congregation and the people he attempts to help. There is no sexual energy associated with it, so there is no confusion in those who are the recipients of the message. (This is, unfortunately, abused by many people who use it to create an attachment to their message, and then eventually an attachment to them).

Philial love is felt between a mother and child, or a brother and sister. It is also the love felt between neighbors and friends. These friendships are stronger than any bond. Any relationship grown in this soil will be a lasting one. As the romantic love recedes, this is the love which holds the relationship together.

Eros is a fire. It boils, but often runs out of steam. It burns itself out. Attraction has one purpose in a natural setting, and that is the manifestation of a child. Eros has many drivers: scent, hormones, physical instincts, psychological imprinting, and imagination. All of these are short term, and are often discarded when the person has outgrown it, grown bored, or has chosen to move on. Unless it is replaced by Philial love, the relationship is doomed. We all say, "I'll love you forever", and that is the first sign of Eros having its way with us. Unfortunately, we all want Eros to last, but it doesn't.

Most people are seeking Eros, because its instantly recognizable, its passionate, sexually charged, and fills the mind and body with a huge amount of endorphines and chemicals. Its addictive.

When I am involved in courting a woman, I seek a philial relationship first, for several reasons. I need to determine if this person is a good match for me intellectually and emotionally. I want to know that they are similar to me, and not going to try to change me. I want a long term relationship, so I look for people with a similar nature, similar goals, similar wants, similar lifestyle, etc.

The term, "Just friends" is a good thing - I'd not have it any other way. I am not looking for a lustful fling. When it is said to a person expressing Eros, it kills them, shatters their vision of what is going on. When it is said to a person who is expressing Philias, it is a good thing, and shows that they are on the path to a great relationship. When it is said to a person who is expressing Agape, their reaction is usually, "Yes, of course. So what?"

Okay, love, I'm long winded. You've inspired me, yet again.

Robert

PS: Have I lead you on in any way? I certainly hope not. You are a wonderful person, and I'd hate to have you think that I'm so common as to be merely in Eros with you.

...
...
...

Chapter Three - A Letter

M.

The things that piss us off the most are often the things we are trying to resolve in our own behavior. That, to my understanding, is projection.

In our brief conversation of last night, I got that things tend towards the same outcome in your personal relationships because you are looking for something specific - somewhat too specific. And whenever you hit a bump in the road, you bail.

I think that you are trying to get perfection on the first try, and need to be willing to accept what is now, and move towards a perfect relationship, as a partner, with the person who you may be with.

Its nice to say that someone is playing "victim", but we are all victims in that we are all reacting to people from our past, and not to the people directly in front of us.

One of the most frequent discussions we have in regards to this, is that most of the men who seem interested in you are substance abusers, or alcoholics. What is it in your behavior that attracts these particular people?

Liars tend to piss you off the most - perhaps it might be wise to ask yourself, why do they lie? In one case, its defensive, in another case, its trying to prop up their broken ego. The latter we generally try to stay away from (instead of calling them on their bullshit - they already know it, there's no use in retaliating with hard words, they're already humiliated enough). In the former, we need to ask ourselves if the lie is trouble enough to deal with. Are they covering up something potentially dangerous (such as a substance abuse problem)?

Or are they merely feeling defensive because they (or their belief systems) feel attacked?

I've recently written to a friend that the greatest relationships start off as a friendship, not as a sexual attraction. Attraction and passion die out - its a fire that burns itself out - if there is a friendship there to begin with, the relationship will have the tools it needs to get through any problem, and overcome them. If there is no friendship there to begin with, the relationship is lost when the passion dies out. Often people try to keep this passion going through arguments, fighting, or by creating drama. Yes, I am guilty of this as well.

Friendship requires a deeper level of respect than most relationships have. A relationship built on respect and mutual understanding has the ability to grow together, because ultimately the soil it is grown in is love.

I love you, my friend.

Robert

...

...

...

I can't believe in you if you keep letting me down.

I've started my 33rd year crying. My 32nd year was far from satisfactory. Loss. Sadness. Looking back at my life I've never been anywhere because I've always had somewhere to go. Something has been eating away at me for so long. I don't really know who or what I am.

I thought today I'd write of those I have loved and lost. There are many and few. There are some more outstanding than others. Some who only dwelt in my heart a short time, then vanished as quickly as they appeared, and some who will remain with me forever as they were. Some I was merely fond of, a brief joy in their company, and some whose presence remained with me for decades. There are some whose names I remember, and some whose faces I remember but whose names were not so driven as deeply into the depths my memory. Remembering some brings tears to my eyes, some a smile. A few have left their mark forever. Yes, love, you have affected me deeply. And some have left scars. Some of these scars are deeper than the names and faces that effected them.

My love is a superficial love, though, because I do not love myself that deeply. I have never believed myself worthy of love, and therefore do not feel it - do not trust it when it is shown to me.

Yes, I am blessed with the love I have received, but I am afraid of love. I have been abandoned too often by those who promised to love me forever and without condition. I do not blame my wife for leaving me. How could she have stayed with someone who would not be loved, no matter how hard she tried? No love is good enough for someone who does not trust it. My God, but I want to feel love. I yearn for nothing more deeply than to feel true love - true heartfelt caring. I do not trust it because it is a crutch. The way of the world is change, and love is not real - if it were, we could not betray it. Love, to be real, to be the greatest force in the universe, needs to be complete, truly overwhelming to that which may oppose it. And how could love betray itself? How is it that love could oppose itself?

So, as I end this 33rd birthday, I cry in the hands of a woman that I care for, who I would love to love, as I think about all of the pains I have done to the world - to the people I loved in this world, and realize that there is no truth, there is no love, there is no peace, there is no joy, there is no final solution, except as the mind makes it so. We all live in a world of our own making. I only want it all, the world is not enough. No matter how much of the world I have, my greed cannot be fulfilled. I am as I am, infinitely deep in the solitude of my aloneness. I am lost, there is no grace. I am lost. If peace find me, it will be in my grave.

As Paulo Coelho wrote, "Suddenly, for a fraction of a second, we feel that our whole life is justified, our sins forgiven, and that Love is still the strongest force, one that can transform us forever." This is what I seek. It is my unicorn.

...

...

...

The loves. Those blessed women who each have a chain wrapped around my heart in some sick fashion. I could not move on from any of them, so true to my word to love them forever might be. Shall I move forwards or back in time?

The first was a little girl. I don't remember her name. I was four or five years old at the time, and our parents used to joke that we'd make a great couple when we were older, promising that they'd marry us off when we grew up. She was pretty, blonde, curly curly hair, and soft blue eyes rimmed by sweet blonde eyelashes. The last time I saw her, we kissed on the step of the Greyhound station. Her parents were moving somewhere. After they left, we went to A&W

where I feasted on onion rings and swore I'd never forget her. So far I've kept my promise.

Three sisters, Brandy, Moosy, and Leslie. There is a strange uniting bond amongst us that still ripples across our lives today, though I have not seen nor heard from them since I was four and a half years old. The five of us were molested by the same people at the same time. These three sweet little girls are probably as insane as my siblings and I are now, and hav likely gone through much of the same heartaches and grief that we went through in our own lives. Brandy was always so shy, and knew better than the rest of us. She had a sharper wit, and I believe she was older than I was. Our babysitters were always trying to coerce her into kissing and such. She wouldn't have anything to do with it. Leslie was a little head case, and already as insane as I was. We'd kiss in the car while our parents stayed in the house drinking. She's the one I'm most afraid for, for already then, at such a young age, she was opened up to the realities of sexuality. Regardless of what people say, there is no healing for those kinds of wounds. They are ingrained into the mind. Moosey would kiss anyone, telling them she loved them. In my later years I learned that this was a sign of molestation or abandonment. I learned one day during harvest season that they went away because their father was molesting them. The poor girls got it from all sides – there was no safety for them. We left shortly thereafter as well, following a similar incident that happened to us. That kind of shit stays with you forever.

Melinda was a little girl whose parents knew my mom. We pretended to get married once, behind the lumber yard one summer day. She ended the wedding by kissing the guy who was being the priest. He was twelve, we were about seven or eight.

Patsy was a little girl who was the sister of my friends down the road. She used to like playing in the garage with me. Her older sister liked kissing my cousin, but somehow believed that kissing meant licking each other's faces. Strange kid. Her brothers were always getting into every kind of trouble, and I was warned off of them a million times by my over protective aunt. She was probably right, but there's not much I can say about that. She was insane in her own way.

Dreams

Turning back the clock,
Pulling at the hands of time
Sands slipping between my fingers,
Dredging up these memories of mine.

I'd rather live in the world
Of my own making
Dreaming of someone
Who was not there for the taking

You cannot ignore me
When I am sleeping,
The only happy endings
Are when I am dreaming.

What makes the surface ripple
Across the sleeping mind
Is it the waves of a new day
Or the hammer striking the chime?

Because I cannot hold you
When I wake to the sun,
I go back to sleep,
And dream another one.

Because in my sleep you are there
Holding me my head against your breast,
Is it only wishful thinking
That I could be with you again.

In my dreams it is always summer,
In my dreams I don't need to eat,
In my dreams you are with me,
In my dreams I can feel your heat.

In my dreams I'm someone special
In my dreams I'm holding tight
In my dreams I'm with you, my love,
In my dreams, every night.

Can you love me like this when I wake,
Can you hold me close, in life?
Can you love me when I'm not dreaming,
Could you be my wife?

If not, I have no reason to wake,
I have no reason to live among
The grains of sand, the seeds of time
The grapes of wrath, the golden sun.

Tell me love, is there any use,
Of living outside my mind?
When someone draws the curtains
On an unfulfilling life.

The Gift of Friendship, The Gift of Love.

"This is yours. No one can take it from you. No one can steal it. I offer it with the deepest humility and gratitude. It has a meaning deeper than anything I could buy you, and more sentimental than anything I could make you. It is neither symbolic nor is it representative of anything. I love you, and care deeply for your well being. I want you to experience happiness in all things. I want to help you realize your dreams. I offer my hand of friendship to you, and I will never retract my love for anything that you may say, do, or think. It is yours to do with as you like. There is no price tag attached to it. There are no expectations involved - be as you are, who you are, and however you want to be. I accept you without the need to change you. If you want to change yourself, I'll be there to help and encourage you, but not to force you into some preexisting idea or mold that I have of you."

I have been learning the meaning of, "unconditional love", that is, love offered without concern over its having been reciprocated or returned. Love offered unconditionally means that, even if a person does not think, speak, or behave in a way that we appreciate, that we may still feel for them the caring that they deserve as a human being. Because I have a desire to improve the world for all humanity, I have the desire to improve the world for every part of that humanity. A mentor of mine once said, "Love is." In spite of the fact that people may despise someone enough to say that they 'hate' that person, often it's the behavior that person has used in expressing themselves that makes them angry and hateful. In other circumstances, we may have forgiven them, wished to help them, even offered them our assistance or advice.

Unconditional love separates the person from their actions, ideas, or words. Love is not removed from the person as a punishment, even though a person may choose to distance themselves from an abusive or dangerous behavior.

Harold Becker, founder of The Love Foundation, describes unconditional love as, "an unlimited way of being... it is the greatest power known to man is that of unconditional love. Through the ages, mystics, sages, singers and poets all expressed the ballad and call to love. As humans, we searched endlessly for the experience of love through the outer senses. Great civilizations have come and gone under the guise of love for their people. Religions have flourished and perished while claiming the true path to love. We, the people of this planet, may have missed the simplicity of unconditional love. ... Simply stated, unconditional love is an unlimited way of being. We are without any limit to our thoughts and feelings in life and can create any reality we choose to focus our attention upon. The qualities of love are endless and the expressions are infinite. The power of unconditional love is within each of us."

As humans, we are constantly seeking to be fulfilled by love, often without realizing that we could never be fulfilled by another, that love from without can only be experienced through the lens of the love which is within, an unconditional love for oneself. The more love we feel for ourselves, the more we are able to resonate with the love from others. Without this self-love, a person may never truly feel loved by his friends and family at all, regardless of how much they may express it. Once a person is able to feel love for them self unconditionally, they will begin to feel love for others unconditionally. This overflow of love is called by many teachers by its Greek name, AGAPE.

Terrible things happen to people, often at the hands of others. There are people who do not know how to express themselves, or whose situations have forced them into a lifestyle or position that may be dangerous or detrimental to others. Over the years, I have come to accept that people may say or do things which may hurt or undermine my feelings, but I often have to look at what the underlying message may be. "You're fat", may mean that they care about my health, and care enough about me to wish that I would take better care of myself. "You're a jerk", could mean that they are trying to get me to pay attention to what I say, how I say it, or who I say it to. These things may not be the healthiest or most considerate ways of expressing love, but there is an underlying meaning to them that, when considered in the light of unconditional love, means that deep down they do care.

From my own experience from having been an abandoned child, I discovered many years later the lessons I had learned from my mother, who was not emotionally or financially stable enough to care for me. Her leaving me to fend for myself in the world taught me to be more resourceful than most people, able to rely on myself, and as a result, to keep myself safe in otherwise terrible circumstances. In addition to this, as well, she was protecting me from her lifestyle, as well as from herself. As I grew older, I felt abandoned, frustrated that I was unloved by her, when in reality, she loved me enough to leave me in the hands of the people she felt that might do a better job in caring for me. Although it took many years for me to make this realization, I have since thanked her for it, and accepted the gift in the spirit with which it was given, even if neither of us realized it at the time.

As I have come to teach people, one must first begin by becoming the change they want to see in the world. By expressing love for oneself, we are then able to begin expressing love for others, without attachment for what they might say or feel, think or do. I have counseled couples by explaining it to them in this way, "Before speaking, first, feel the emotion that you want them to feel. When you talk, this emotion will come out in your facial features, voice tones, choice of words, and your body language."

We are thinking machines. We are all learning, growing, expanding our awareness, educating ourselves. The only real constant in this universe it that it will change, everything changes. Once we understand this fact, we are able then to understand that people can and will change in time. "I accept you as you are, on your way to something better." When I was in high school, I was the kid who nobody liked, who was constantly picked on by the bigger kids. As an adult, going back home, I ran into a couple of these boys, now grown up, who somehow remember being very fond of me. They asked after my family, got to know me as an adult, and we were able to go for beers together and became close friends. When I brought up the fist fights and the pranks they pulled on me, we were able to laugh it off as the childish antics they were.

"Agape is total love, the love that devours those that experience it. Whoever knows and experiences Agape sees that nothing else in this world is of any importance, only loving."

- Paulo Coelo, the Pilgrimage

DOM SLK - 11:37

Faking peace like a renegade
I'm more than you can handle,
I'll stick your head above my mantle
You'll go up like a hand grenade
You think that there's a scandal,
I'll go off like a roman candle.

You think you got me, though,
I'll slaughter y'all
I'll cut off your balls
And feed them to the gulls.

Little Man, you think you're dangerous,
You're only slanderous,
You're tongue can't handle us,

I'll cut you up like a magazine,
I'll make you scream,
I'll rob you clean,
Don't think I'm a murderer?
I'll scalp and torture you.
I'll take your fingers, too.
I'll bag you till your face turns blue.

You're going to beg, boy
For me to let you go,
We're not going to speak a word,
Watch, I'll tell you so.
You won't know what hit you, fool,

With no eyes, tongue or fingers
I'll leave you with the pain that lingers,
You won't know what to do.

I can wait a million years,
Until the pain of waiting brings on tears
No one will be missing you,
Believe you - me, no one cares.

Note:

There's only pain in Rap. Love is for the dead and
dying. Peace is for the weak. Murder your neighbor,
makes you a hero in the hood, son.

My Darkest Angel

Cassandra, you were there with me
Listening to my sobs,
Holding me when I cried
In my darkest hour of need.

You listened with hungry ears
With no words to console me
I loved you in that moment
In your young and tender years.

When you are leaving me again
What hope is there for us?
When all things have passed away
What things for us remain?

Driven on by the touch
Of your skin, your hands, your face
I think again of your loving heart
I think of you too little, too much.

Another Rhyme. I hate Rhymes

I have moved on and changed my name
On my hands are golden chains
I have taken on a brand new game
On my back are angel's wings

If you were to know me now
You may not recognize who I am.
If you were to see that now
I've traded the wolf for the ram.

I am creating a brand new face,
I dance alone under laughing stars.
I am the solstice sun rising in grace,
I am the faith of the priest at work.

I wish you to see the king I've become,
To see the sun that guides my hand,
To see the work that I've begun.
And still you think of me as I was.

Awaken, dear sister, awaken my love,
To salvage this wasteland of our lives.
Awaken, my children, there's time enough
To open our hearts, to open our eyes.

Stanzas for Cathrine

A child's life ruined by tragedy
Abandoned, torn and jaded
By life's mysterious way of things.

Did you forget that we lived and loved
Did you know that we endured together
Those things that keep you awake?

When we grew older, I thought I rose above
Those things we carried with us,
To discover that they tainted my life, too.

You carried the shit in your life,
I thought myself above such conditioning,
Only to find them skip a generation.

So here we are, dear little sister,
Four Generations in the making,
Tied to the cross, Tied to the wheel.

Carrying the tragedy with us each day,
Without awareness of it's impact,
We cannot break free, we cannot break free.

Notes:

I am so fucked up over the patterns I see in our generational karma. Our grandmother and her abandonment of our mother, our mother's abandonment of us, and finally, our abandonment of our own children.

I think, ultimately, the difference will be in how we choose to break the cycle - will we finally choose to take the children back and give them the homes and lives they deserve? Can we break that cycle so they don't have to stumble through the same gulag?

There are more patterns than this that are four generations old, abuse, addictions, poverty, etc...but this is the one that is safer to discuss in public.

A Poem for Preston

I'll be the first to admit
That I am hurting those
That I care most about.

I am self centred and absorbed
by my own self destruction
And dragging my friends into it.

I wish I knew how to apologize
In a way that was satisfacory
To a friend who has stood by me.

You told me last that I am wrong
For my perceptions and manners,
And I agree that I probably am

We admire one another
For the people we are
And what we represent.

What that means to me
Is more than mere friend,
It means Brother.

So if you would be so kind
As to catch me when I fall
And forgive me when I'm wrong,

I will do the same for you

If the time comes
To apologize.

I'm sorry.

A Poem for Natalee

You said that I write nothing new,
That it is all the same
Bitter, empty heartache -
I write what I know.

Your suggestion,
and the suggestion of others,
Is that I devote my words
To manifesting what I desire -
Positivity and Joyful thought.
I agree.

I have taken down the portrait
Of my wife and I on the wall,
Where you had commented once
That she didn't care for me
Even then.

It was like tearing a piece
Of myself from the rack
Which I had been torturing
Myself with daily.
You are right.

I pulled down the shrine
With our wedding picture
Surrounded by crystals
And orgone generators -
Dead rememberances.

I hung on to what was left,
Clinging with torn fingernails
To what might remain of her,
Chasing away the memory

Because it was empty.

Perhaps the reality is
That I hang on too much
To that which is lost
Without understanding that
Sometimes there is no meaning.

I cannot seek to replace
Something irreplaceable -
I cannot seek solace
In a world of hurt.
Let it go.

Six months of solitude,
Six months of soul searching
Six months of grieving
For the loss of something
That never really was.

The lesson you have taught me
Is to let go of my illusions,
For nothing is real
Except as the mind
Makes it so.

A Poem for Mandi Schrader

My dear, beloved friend:-
You would have me meditate on what I have
With gratitude and with joy
For what I've accomplished.

I have indeed achieved great things
Though not yet the greatest.
I might have a full life
Fulfilling and abundant
Because I choose to have it
With patience and goodness
Inspired.

The sweat on my brow
Knows the toil of an
Enlightened path
And yet I yearn,
Still I yearn.

I am alone, my love,
As a monk in a cell
Forgotten to his prayers.
We pray for different things,
My spiritual counterpart and I:
I to Mammon, he to Christ,
I beg for an endless shower of gold,
He for a stainless soul.

The path I am on has left me

Battered and frayed,
But still I shine on in the darkness
A twinkling star aglow
With the knowledge that
Thou art with me.

I do not have what I would want,
I do not want what I have,
If I cannot anoint it
With the love of my children
And my wife who had abandoned them.
And yet, it was an empty life, too.

What am I seeking that I cannot find?
Am I blind to the world
That is right there before me?

I spent my yesterday
In silence and meditation
While pious souls
To church and prayed.

What I discovereed there
Was that I am alone,
I cannot love myself
Because I have never known love.
I do not understand it,
I do not know it to see it,
Inspired only by movie pathos
And not by real, genuine joy.

I survive in a world where I was abandoned
By mother, family, friends, lovers.
There is nothing that is permanent,
And that is the key --
I have not yet abandoned myself.

Notes:

Mandi: You're damn right I would! You have an
enviably wondrous life, I maintain.

Joy Joy

Choosing a way to find myself
I am told that there is nothing to find.
You mock me, yet cower
Wondering what I might do
If pushed to far.

I am empty,
Willing to remain half full
For at least that is something.

No regrets, just an empty billfold
Searching for an excuse
To stay clean.

Yea, though I walk in the shadow
Of the Valley of the Dead,
I shall fear no evil
For there is naught to fear
Of those already having passed.

I do not fear the living
Because I know they have already
Taken from me what they can.

I am a man of many talents,
A man of many words,
A man without purpose
Easily abused and conspired against.
Take from me what you will,

I know that they can be replaced,
Those little things that do not matter -

But you chose to take from me
Everything that mattered the most,
And thought you might do so with impunity.
Do you really think me so easily destroyed?

I burn you with every thought
I bind you with every deed
I banish you with every word.
You are nothing
You have nothing

Spirit of the Earth, Remember!
Spirit of the Sky, Remember!

You gods of little faith,
You spirits everlasting
You who would have my prayers
Answer with little more than
Emptyness.

Tuberculosis

There was once a time when I loved the world
And wished for sunshine and roses for all.

Then the sun stopped shining and the roses died,
And all that was left was dirt and ash.

But from dirt and ash rises new life
From the rains which pour from sadness

For without one we cannot have the other,
For without pain there is no pleasure.

These Aeons

I spent some time
With an amazing woman
And Life was good
For Once.

But things fall apart
As often they do
Change is the only
Constant.

The ebb and flow
Of the universes toil
Will wax and wane
Eventually

I have come to accept
We sleep in the beds
Of our own making
Finally.

But all this as well
Will come to pass
And be forgotten to
Oblivion

Our lives are as
We make them
One moment at a
Time.

One day we will die
And be lost to history
Unimportant, unremembered
Forgotten.

The Left Hand Path

I would that I could love you
That life would be joyous each day.
I would that I could hold you,
Loving you in every way.

That I would do anything for you
Need not be required to show
My love to the letter, each sentence,
If only so that you might know.

There are a thousand things here
That I might do to prove you my love,
But affection and salvation aside
A thousand things may not be enough.

You see, you are seeking something
That I do not seem to have within me.
You are seeking something trivial,
Something superficial, something skin deep.

If you were worthy of my love,
You might seek something deeper,
Something meaningful, something real,
Something loftier, something ethereal.

I see in your eyes the fear of a hopeless life,
I see in you something that you fear to live,
I see in you the wish for love everlasting,
I see in you something greater than a wife.

Dirty Laundry

I have been accused of this once before, so I will make plain my feelings on the matter.

I am a writer. I write. I despise confrontation, as too oft it turns to arguement with unneccessary loops of logic which draw in logical fallacy and misdirection.

When I write, it is for the world inasmuch as it is for myself.

I have been accused that my writing is passive agressive. Passive-aggression is typically obstructionist resistance to following through with certain expectations, manifested as procrastination, stubbornness, resentment, sullenness, or repeated failure to accomplish requested tasks.

I'm quite certain that my writing is none of these.

I have been accused in the past that my writing is obscure -- meaning that people don't "get it" as readily as they'd like. Obviously, the audience may need to look more deeply in the writer's point of reference than in their own.

I write in terms of my life. There is no attack on particular people - crass as it may seem, I will not openly force attention on another person, only on the behavior they have displayed. It is not for me to make anyone out to be an enemy or a "bad guy". I do not name names. One cannot throw mud without getting their own hands blackened. If a person in my audience notices a reflection of themselves in what has been written, that is their own prejudice. I have not dirtied my laundry by smearing theirs.

Read, or don't read. It matters not to me what you see in the mirror, only that you bother to look within it deeply enough to see the writer's world within it. If you see yourself, you are not looking deeply enough. If you take offense to what is written there, then perhaps the writer has accomplished something in evoking a feeling of pathos - whatever that pathos may be. Hate me, love me, but don't accuse me of what you see there.

Notes:

Consequently, I am, as a reasonable human being, fully capable of loving and respecting a person even though they may think, do and say things that I don't agree with.

One should never mistake the act with the person.

That's Just The Way I Am.

There was once a little boy named Bobby who had no friends. He didn't know anybody, and wasn't going to be staying long. He had no toys, and no one to talk to.

One day, Bobby was playing on the front step of the place his parents had rented, when he met a boy from down the street, named Lenny. Lenny asked if Bobby would like to play a game. "Sure", he said.

Lenny picked up a handful of stones, and to Bobby's horror, Lenny threw the largest one at Bobby's dad's car. It chipped the paint on the hood. "What the hell are you doing?" Bobby screamed. "Having fun. What do you think?" Lenny replied, calm, a look of indifference on his face. Bobby reached to stop him from grabbing more stones, and Lenny punched him in the lip, threw a handful more at the car, and ran away.

Bobby cried after him, "Why?"

Lenny yelled over his fleeting shoulder, "That's just the way I am."

* * *

Bob was in the high school english class, the second last day before Christmas break. Many of the kids around him were taking part in creating snowflakes and other mindless crafts for the school play. Bob was finishing his homework, which had lapsed a bit from his time in the hospital - two weeks behind, and upset that no one had asked if he was okay.

Shane, a pug nosed creature of sluggish stature and vile demeanor walked over to Bob's table, and threw a handful of paper confetti at him, smiling in his brutish way.

Bob calmly dusted himself off, avoiding a confrontation, and brushed the paper dots aside with his arm. Shane answered by throwing another handful at Bob, the footballers in the corner sniggering. Bob again brushed the confetti aside, but this time placed the pile of paper bits on a piece of paper, rolled it up, and blew it like a trumpet in Shane's face.

Shane jumped over the table and punched Bob in the lip. Bob got on top of Shane and blackened his eye. The footballers grabbed them both and held them seperate.

In the next class, Shane and the footballers sniggered in the corner, threatening to "get him" after school. Bob said, "okay" and waited at the doors by the gymn after class.

Behind the gymn, hundreds of kids had gathered, all of them cheering for Shane.

Shane came tumbling towards Bob with his fists clenched at his sides. Bob broke his nose before he had a chance to raise them. Shane went down in a pile of snow. Bob kicked him repeatedly in the ribs. Again the footballers picked Bob up off of Shane's bloody mess and pushed him away. Bob's hand were cold.

After the police cruiser left the school, and everyone went home, Shane's big brother - the footballer that pulled Bob off of Shane, asked "Why?" Bob replied, "He'll never do it again. Bullies don't deserve respect, nor do they deserve mercy. That's just the way I am."

* * *

Rob's sixteenth birthday came and went, with no presents, no friends, and no birthday wishes. His mother left a half smoked pack of cigarettes and an empty lighter on his dresser, but he was sure it was just forgotten there earlier - not actually a gift.

Three days went by, and still no one thought of him - no cake, no respect, no remorse. His sister arrived with a new boyfriend in tow behind her. "This is Nelson", she said, "He's got something for you." Nelson held up a small pillowcase, inside of which were three gifts, each neatly wrapped, each with a small bow, and a small ribbon. Each gift had a name tag which read, "Happy Birthday, Bobby" on it.

Rob opened the first gift. Inside was a gorgeous Rolex watch, gold accented with platinum, a diamond stud marking each hour. Rob opened the second gift. Inside was a large ruby ring, the square stone encompassed in bright gold, inside the band was the inscription, "Happy Birthday". Rob opened the third gift. Inside was a leather wallet with a fifty dollar bill inside. Rob looked up with tear soaked eyes and said, "Thank you."

The next day at school, Rob was called into the office. The two police officers asked him where he had gotten the watch, ring and wallet. "I found them", he said. When his cell mate asked him why he didn't rat out his sister, he replied, "That's just the way I am."

* * *

Robert was married to the most amazing woman he had ever met. Her smile filled his heart with a glee he had never known before. She ran her fingers through his hair and held him from behind. She whispered to him how much she loved him and how happy she was.

When she asked for a divorce, he asked her why. Her answer was clear, "That's just the way I am."

* * *

The soul looked at the series of events in its life, the good, the bad, the indifferent. The judge looked down upon it and asked, "How do you plead?"

"That's just the way I am."

I am not I

I have not written in so long, my fingers itch.

Where am I, where have I been,

Cut loose, wandering the streets

Wishing for a home.

You have not held me in trust

You have not held me dearly as you should have.

There is no peace. No option. No remorse.

I wish I could cut it loose,

But I cannot, it is all I have.

The memory. Faded.

The Socialist Corporation of Canada

Love, Compassion, and Truth – these are my law. You will not find them in any of your law books. You will not find these laws supported by your corporate government.

I have had two arguments today, both of which I feel that I have won. In the first, I was told that I have no right to bitch about what the government does if I have not voted. There is an obvious logical fallacy here, because the government will do whatever it wants to, regardless of whether or not you win the vote. You are voting for a representative, nothing more. That person will represent you in their meetings, your voice counts only if it is heard. Why is it then that atrocities are committed in your name? Why is it that you would allow these atrocities to continue? You voted for that representative, that representative voted to kill babies in your name. Thereby, you are a baby-killer. No one will kill anyone in my name – ever.

The second argument had to do with government funding of the arts. Now, anyone who knows me also knows that I am a capitalist – not a corporatist – I believe in responsibility, not limited liability. As a capitalist, I believe that a person should be able to take care of themselves in as much as they are capable. Socialist governments believe in giving away money and support in trade for freedom. They will cause a person to beg for assistance, and with the right hand take away freedom, while with the left giving whatever was asked for (often less than was asked for, and usually after making you feel like a shit for asking in the first place).

I pay for my health insurance. I pay for my car insurance. Thereby I have taken care of my responsibilities in any instances where these assurances are needed to protect my own or someone else's welfare. I did not go to the government to beg for cheaper rates or better returns on my insurance investment. I take responsibility for my own mistakes, and do not expect other people to have to shoulder the burden.

I told her that I am more than happy to help those who ask me to help them, so she responded, "I need $2000 for my art show". I answered that I don't have $2000, but I'd be more than willing to help her find it, to sell some paintings for her, perhaps even to buy a couple myself. I'd host an art show on her behalf, and maybe find her some way to make money quickly in order to fund the show. She said that she could do that herself, and I said that, "Smart money works harder than struggling money. If you were able to do it yourself, you wouldn't be asking." She argued that there is money in the government to pay for this sort of thing, and I said that I didn't believe in money that is not EARNED. I said that my method of funding her show would be more difficult, that there would be work involved. She began to cry. Apparently this is not what she wanted to hear.

I started my publishing company with a infinitesimal $5.00 investment. Five bucks, and lots of hard work. Its paid off in huge ways. I now own several successful companies, and just purchased another successful company. I am successful because I didn't go asking for handouts. Yes, I took loans, for which I am personally liable, but they are being paid back, with interest.

Don't give up your freedom. Be a sovereign person – if you can't do something yourself, then its not worth it. Add value to the community; don't decrease the value to yourself by begging for success. Earn it.

PART TWO

Fragments

2002 - 2005

Preface

The following section is drawn from fragments and writing from the period of 2002 – 2005. Most of the text is taken from newsletters, essays, articles, and short stories. The excerpts and fragments are from several sources.

The Seeds of Life

I am grateful for this day, for I know that my accomplishments are not yet fulfilled, and that I may use this moment to work towards my goals. I am prepared to do what must be done, with vigor and with joy.

I release yesterday, with its trials and tragedies, frustrations and aggravations, its setbacks and angers. The past does not dictate the actions of the present, nor the course of the future. I will make amends for anyone I have done wrong, and will work towards perfecting my thoughts, my words, and my behaviors.

I will treasure this moment, for it is all that I have. I will not concern myself with a past I cannot change, nor with a future I cannot experience. The past is done, the future will take care of itself. My only concern is what I do with now. Regret for the past and fear for the future will only hinder the work of the present.

I will face the challenges of the day with resolve and confidence, for I am assured in my success with every action I take towards my goals. As I live in the moment, my food will be fully tasted, my water completely refreshing, the more satisfying will be my sleep, and the more fully will I live. I am free from the slavery of other people's expectations.

I will practice patience and benevolence, peace and charity. I am aware of how little it takes to remain completely satisfied with the day. I do not have to pursue happiness, for I have attained it at every moment, all I need do is to notice it. I do not have to pursue enlightenment, for I am enlightened here and now, all I need do is to realize it.

I will face my fears and the dangers I am faced with, because

I am certain that with every challenge that I am confronted with, I am able to discern an appropriate solution. It is through the days adversities that I will become more than I am now.

I release everyone I meet today from my expectations, and wrap them in unconditional acceptance. I know that the seeds of conscious thought form the basis of my behavior, and that this in turn will affect the events of the day, the behaviors of others, and the course of my future.

These seeds I sow in the fertile soil of the mind will always be harvested, for good or ill. And so, I will sow good thoughts, good ideas, and positive beliefs, for even if they are not manifested immediately, they offer more solace than a thought contrived from fear, anger, or confusion. If life is experienced in this manner, it will bear fruits of beauty and wonder. If life is experienced with ignorance and close-mindedness, it will only produce ignorance and close-mindedness.

Throughout the day I will condition myself to manage every problem I encounter as a wonderful opportunity to improve myself and my skills, and I will face the challenge with confidence and enthusiasm. The universe is a mirror of the soul, and so I will face it with a smile, regardless of the pain I may feel, knowing that ultimately I will reap the rewards of the seeds that I sow. I will make decisions with these conditions in mind, and to the best of my abilities.

I will not follow temptations for things which may be harmful to my honor, my health, my self-esteem, or my self-respect. At the end of the day, I will look at these temptations as a test of my character, a test which can only strengthen my will, my personality, and my powers of discernment. I will turn every sorrow into joy, every grief into growth, and every challenge to an advantage, for I know that every small accomplishment only betters the world, not only for myself, but for others as well.

I may not realize the greater significance of my actions, but I will attempt to improve it for everyone involved or affected by them. These are the seeds of life that I sow this day, and every day. I am thankful for the opportunity to take part in a life less ordinary!

Astrophel

Chapter One

"There are many events in the womb of time which will be delivered upon you. An intelligent man is observant of spirit, but a wiser man is observant of his ear, and perceives the serpent's tongue where it is most likely to cause a vulgar thought."

- Frater Ego Esse

The sun rose over the windowsill, shining full on Astrophel's face as the alarm woke him from his sleep. "Good morning", he whispered, stretching the life back into his limbs. He could smell coffee rising on the air from downstairs, and climbed out of his bed. He could hear the sounds of his room-mates coming to life as he washed quickly, looked out at the cold autumn sky. "Looks like its going to be a brisk one", he said to the walls, as he took out his clothing and prepared for the day ahead.

Situated in a large Victorian house, his apartment consisted of a bedroom, study, and bathroom. He shared the kitchen and common with four other students, each quite intelligent in their respective fields, and each getting along rather well with each other. The rental of the house was a common effort, and the tenants proved themselves to be responsible and dependable.

Astrophel took to the floor, sitting in a manner common only to those to whom meditation is practiced religiously. Coffee would have to wait, and it usually did. Kneeling on the floor with his feet tucked under his body,

Frater Astrophel began to breathe deeply, counting to four as he inhaled, held his breath for four, exhaled for four, and held again in the same manner. This cyclic breath continued unceasing for thirty minutes, all the while his body controlled, his thoughts becoming less and less random, his mind trained upon the count between his breaths. He allowed no other thoughts to intrude, as he had done every morning for ten years. As he finished his meditation, the stretched again in a series commonly called the Sun Salutation, and went to breakfast.

Coffee did indeed wait, and his flat mates were kind enough to leave him toast, eggs, and a slice of bacon besides. When the meal was finished, and Astrophel removed all trace of the morning's repast, he returned to his room.

One is often surprised at Frater Astrophel's spartan existence. Most who have met him expected a life of eclectic affluence. Although his tastes were, in fact, more towards simple elegance, he never revealed himself to be anything more than a humble creature. Never was a word spoken of his endeavors in the mystical, and his room was never shared by more than his own small library of select manuals, his chest of magickal regalia, and a writing desk. He did not spend his money rashly, nor did he speak of his accomplishments or his effects. He chose his words most carefully, and this, when combined with his firm gaze and soft manner, created a personality that attracted the honest and banished the weak minded and foolhardy.

Astrophel was a writer, and never took credit for his own work. Not many people had ever read his books, and he never promoted them except in classified advertisements and letters to a variety of bookstores. He made a modest living, and his lifestyle required much less than he made. He shared his earnings with his mother, who lived across the country where the weather was more satisfactory to her health conditions, and he kept the remainder carefully concealed in a worn copy of the Gideon Bible. He never counted it, but knew that it was a significant amount. He was never found wanting, and indeed, was often able to afford himself simple luxuries, such as a beautiful felt overcoat and a small collection of leather bound journals, into which he wrote his revelations.

"Wednesday", he said to himself, and glanced at his schedule, which read a coffee meeting with his friend Albus the Priest and dinner with a brief acquaintance, a young girl named Vaughn, who had taken an arbitrary sort of fondness for him.

Astrophel sat at his desk, opened his personal ledger, and began to stare at the sheet, his mind clearing and his hand resting softly upon the page. As he stared at the vellum, a beautiful handwriting began to appear upon the page, floating softly in light grey ink, forming the next lines to his manuscript:

"Visualize yourself as a young carpenter, hands toughened by a lifetime of labor, mind sharpened to a fine point, eyes that are able to discern the length, shape and angle of an object by its very appearance. You are as you think you are, and the skills of the imagined woodcarver are now yours, synchronous and wrought smoothly into your own."

As his mind opened to allow the lines to unfold before him as a fine illumination, he traced over the hallucination, and the words in ink remained to be shared with those who might feel compelled to read them.

"These same hands, made used to honest work, also understand the meaning of gesture and symbol. As the simple carpenter realizes that his trade earns him his body's nourishment, he also understands that the lessons learned him through mystical practice may also reveal the spiritual nourishment required to maintaining a healthy and enlightened mind."

The letters filled the page with an ink only Astrophel might see, and these he revealed with his stylus, ink rolling smoothly onto the pages. Just as Amadeus Mozart could imagine entire scores in his head as he wrote them, so too could Astrophel imagine entire books printed on the page before him.

The words scrolled over the pages, one word at a time, as if some unseen hand wrote them upon the page. Astrophel was amazed that, upon a moment's reflection, he was on his thirtieth page, the time passing such that it was nearly time to leave to meet the Priest. Quickly, he scanned over the pages, and upon the last page, which read:

"The hands that wrought harmonic measures within the wood might also fashion harmonic measures in the souls of mankind. There is nothing more universal in the awakened mind than the discovery that any structure in the cosmos has its parallels within other structures, and that the nature of this arrangement is a common bond within the harmonics of that family. What is known of one thing is known of another, and for the initiate who regards the hand as a figure of harmonic ratios and structure, so too will that initiate discover that all of *nature contains that same structure: the measures of the body, the curve of the nautilus, the numbers of generative sequences, and the lengths between the points of a pentagram."*

The air was cold, and Astrophel kept his hands hidden in the folds of his overcoat, his boots crunching over the frost on the sidewalk overlooking the river. The house was thirty blocks from the Fauno Ebbrio Coffeehouse, but only a twenty minute walk away. He concentrated upon the scent of the air, the crisp outline of each form within sight, and the sounds of the city around him. Awareness of the moment was easily sustained for him, as he had practiced mindfulness for nearly ten years, never allowing his mind to wander, bringing it gently back to the task at hand, which was to experience the moment fully, without judgment or internal comment.

As he entered the Café, the air thick with perfumed smoke and filled with the scent of espresso and incense. The faces were familiar, the Gothic crowd of beautifics and trend-hippies, masquerading as if Halloween were a daily event. There is a singular irony in collective individuality. Albus sat in the corner, his priestly regalia melding with the monochromatic crowd, inseperate from their statement.

"Ave Frater."

"Salve." Astrophel removed his jacket, laying it against the sofa by the little coffee table in the corner. Typical new millennia style, mismatched furniture and local indie artwork upon the walls. "How are you? I haven't seen you for weeks now. Anything new I should know about?" They shook hands over the coffee table, Frater Albus' silver ring of his office flashing in the muted light.

"We'll be meeting for mass again on Wednesday night, if you're wont to join us", was the simple reply, filled with a bored discontent. This was a conversation which took place far too often between the two men, and it rarely led to Astrophel's involvement in the Gnostic church's exercise.

"We'll see what presents itself in the mean-time. How is your lady?" A stunning fact of heresy to most, Albus was a married man, and loved as he lived - in the world but not of it.

"She's well." He paused, his hand moving to his jacket pocket to reveal a small package. "I've something for you. A gift, from Athanasius."

Athanasius, or Father Tau Malachi, as he was known throughout the Gnostic world, had died over a year ago. His loss was devastating to Astrophel, who revered him like one might a beloved uncle. Athanasius was at one time the Frater Superior of Astrophel's Order, the Angilluminati.

"It is a book, to be given you on your twenty fifth birthday, or your entrance into the degree of Magus. You will be twenty five in six months, and you attained your grade nearly a month ago. I have been busy since. I hope you enjoy, it is a favorite of mine.

The brown wrapping was elegant in its simplicity. The binding was a simple grey-green cloth with a single gold stamp in the center, depicting the eye within the triangle. The octavo was small, but well kept. Within the cover was a small inscription in Frater Athanasius's unmistakable handwriting: "My brother, for brother you now are, whether by degree or by age. You are no longer kept in my service, but are a man of your own making. May this book take you to the next layer of understanding. Do not expect some mystical nonsense within these pages, but only the truth, and even that is but an interpretation for the mind to accept, believe, and then eventually discard. In Lvx, In Vita, In Amare Constantia, Frater Athanasius."

Father Albus had lit a cigarette, another vice for such a virtuous soul. And as this was a non smoking establishment, the powers that be would notice eventually and kindly enforce their restrictions – no tobacco on the premises. Father Albus was never a man of rules.

"What is it?"

"A book of course. You might call it "The Word"."

"A Book of Creation?" Astrophel eyed the book curiously, his interest peaked by its very simplicity.

"Not really, more a Book of Revelation. I will leave much of the reading to you, but if you have any insight, feel free to contact me. As well, you might find the contents very difficult to understand in the context with which it was written. Do not attempt to interpret the information in some metaphorical understanding – it is to be read and understood in as concise a manner as possible."

Father Albus caught the eye of the bartender, who motioned towards the nearly finished cigarette. Albus flicked the remaining ash on the floor, and sent the cigarette hurtling through the air towards the nearby fireplace, crackling against the black backdrop of painted faces and blue-black hair.

Astrophel opened the book to the title page, which read, "There are dangerous books in the world today. Some are known to be inhabited by a demon known as THOUGHT. These books are created with a purpose, instructed with intent, and have lives of their own. Do not inhibit their passage, for their message is often stronger than the hands that would hold them."

* * *

Astrophel carried the book lightly cradled in his gloved hand as he strode towards the golden doors of The Sphinx. This was one of his favorite establishments, quiet, unobtrusive: a hangout for artists and hippies. The pleasant smells of simple food and drink welcomed him as he opened the brass doors, the hinges squeaking gently against the cold night air. A quick look around revealed the usual clientele, and his friend Francis at the bar who waved him in. The mellow sound of a jazz band practicing in the rear of the room licked his ears as he noticed the long brown tresses of Vaughn in the corner of the room, reading a book of poetry.

As he walked towards her, she looked up and smiled, laying the book down carefully on the edge of the table, so as not to lose her page.

"What's new?" He said, hugging her lightly as he sat next to her, facing the room. She looked quite attractive, Latin face, black sweater, latte mulatto. The book found the edge of the table under his arm, and his hand found hers, a subtle caress which often accompanies young courtship.

"Nothing much. I just finished writing the invitations to the Solstice party. I think we'll carry it at Scotchman's Hill, overlooking the river."

"Good idea. I might even show up myself." He laughed, giving her hand a squeeze.

"Well, you know us witches, always wanting to take our clothes off at public events. I'd hate for you to not be there – but I'll make do." She rolled her eyes and smiled.

"You know I'm not into social events, but I'll try to be there. You let me know when and where." He paused to sip his coffee, which Francis brought over, so unobtrusively as to be completely unnoticed, the cup seeming to have materialized of its own accord. "So what are you going to do, some sort of haphazard ritual, designed to scare the halfwits and allow the oldschoolers to feel like they're doing something of real value? Or just a party with a couple of bonfires with the city lights below you?"

"Maybe a little of both. Who knows. The "oldschoolers", as you call them, can rarely agree on a tradition to practice, much less a common purpose to a ritual working." Her eyebrows flickered with momentary frustration, and then her eyes brightened, alighting upon his new volume, nearly hidden under his arm, "What's that!?"

"A gift from my mentor." Astrophel replied, arm not moving from its position, half covering the book. The gold embossed stamp on the cover insisted she touch it, drew her hand closer to its simple elegance, but the look of casual warning on Astrophel's face, and his steadfast position kept her fingers in check, curiosity held at bay by simple will.

"Pretty." She replied. The book's unavailable contents begged her attention, but she forced her bibliophilia to hide beneath a soft grin. There was always time enough for books.

"There are certain things that cannot be shared, even between intimates. I am held by an oath, and not one that I could break without impunity. "

She smiled in understanding

Philosophy of Life   I

Introduction

There are thousands of books discussing religious doctrines, philosophies, commandaries, et cetera. But there are very few which discuss the Philosophy of Life. What is religion except a guide for experiencing life in its fullest and most passionate way possible? Present day religion is filled with such nonsense as fearful futuristic expectations about the "end times" and notions about a jealous and angry "father figure" named God. Worship has been, for many generations, a terrifying experience, based in the attempt by man to appease and control this terrifying omnipresent, omnipowerful deity, to earn its favor with sacrifices, prayer, and worship. Interpretations have become very muddled as the context progresses further from the original intention of scripture. This particular argument, though, is outside the realm of our present text. Our intention here is to outline the variety of statements which have a direct impact on what makes the world a better place for all.

We are of the opinion that there is a particular way to live, to think, and to behave which is both beneficial to the person in becoming more enlightened and able to experience divinity both within and without, to care for the environment for both ourselves and for future generations, and to assist others in awakening to their potential, to help them discover the Philosophy of Life in an unobtrusive and non-interfering manner. Each of these goals is a matter of personal responsibility, and generally uncommon sense. We have become so used to creating a fundamentalist philosophy, rife with "thou shalt not's" and forced reverence for an unknowable God, and a forced Faith in a variety of corrupt organizations, that we have forgotten the real purpose of the philosophies themselves.

It is not our place to argue against such foolish attacks which will be laid against us here, such as those fear-mongers and sellers of hate denouncing the teachings as "New Age", "Satanic", "Heretical", &c. These are precisely the people who would benefit most from learning how to love and trust, to heal and to create. But in present, these victims of close-minded fundamentalism and intolerance must be allowed to suffer their own psycho-sclerosis (hardening of the attitudes). As will be explained later, these are the people who have become so frightened of shadows on the wall that they can no longer experience the light. Those who commit to seek the devil will eventually manifest the devil. It is a brush that will taint even the taste of the food in their mouths.

It is not our intention to direct people to worship in strange and unusual manners, our philosophy as it is discussed here draws upon a variety of manuscripts and teachings, both ancient and recent. There is no place here for discussion of whether or not a teaching comes from an "accepted" source by one denomination or another, as the structure is the same throughout – to direct and guide the reader to a manner of living life in the most wonderful way possible, to make the most of their abilities, and to become more fully human; for it is in this search that we become more than human.

The Philosophy presented here is a culmination of many years of research by many different minds. Our present publication of this research in the Philosophy of Life is an extension of their work, thousands of years worth of effort on the part of many different people, in many different parts of the world, attempting to find a solution to the problem so many have faced: The Purpose and Meaning of Life. Without delving into theories about Divinity or After Life

Experiences, such as Heaven, Hell, Reincarnation, or other abstract concepts that we cannot ourselves immediately verify, we must instead choose to direct our efforts into the realms of the most likely evaluation of our present condition: Life, and the thorough mastery of it.

Much of this information is recognizable, as you may have read the original sources, such as the Christian Bible, the Muslim Koran, or even the writings of poets such as Rumi, Lord Byron, Shakespeare, and many other people who have written down their observations and beliefs. In many cases, these have been paraphrased and reordered, or retranslated to suit our understanding. It is not our place to contemplate the existence of God, Angels, Djinns, Fairies, Elementals, or Thoughtforms. It is instead our opinion that God is described in many different ways by mankind, and it is through these descriptions that we share with each other our beliefs and persuasions. Many of us tend to argue for or against this teaching or that, and forget that different circumstances require a flexible understanding of cause and effect. For example, murder may be a terrible offense, but is considered by many to be the only solution to fascism, terrorism, oppression, and many other crimes against humanity. Theft may be an unfortunate solution to the problem of starvation in some circumstances. In most cases, crimes are justified by the people who take part in them. In some cases, love may be seen as a terrible act, especially between a married person and one who is not her spouse. In other situations, the act of ownership must be called into question where chattel represents slaves, children, or a person's spouse. Much of this relates to the philosophy of Ethics. Ethics is a system of moral principles concerning human behavior, stressing points of an ideology based on good, evil, right, wrong, virtues, vices, standards, and laws. Often, these rules become constrictive themselves, and are often used to justify otherwise unjustifiable behavior by the majority over the few, and the fundamentalist over the more flexible. Opinions will always change regarding the nature of a situation, and it is generally wiser to remain unrestrictive in your views and ideologies.

Please enjoy this collection of Life Philosophies. The ideas provided here are intended to provide you with the tools you will need in changing your attitudes and behaviors in such a manner as to enhance your experience of life.

In Lvx,
Anon.

Philalethia

It is the wise man who learns from the mistakes of the past, lest he fall to repeating them. Study the pivotal persons in history, search for the commonalities in their behaviors, their personalities, their characters - ask yourself what it is that has made them successful. Seek these keys of phenomenal success and incorporate them into your own behavior. Reach for the secret of miracles, and you will find them.

Great leaders are remembered by record of the things they've said - the legacies they've left behind. These monuments are the grand ideas, the Seeds of truly occult knowledge, for they are what manifest the divine in man. Words are not merely representatives of things, not just symbols. Words can be spoken with vitality, conviction, power, and may carry the full weight of a vision. Words have power to manifest great change when wielded by one who takes care not to abuse them with vulgarity or garrulous behavior. Words are the key to the mind, and the power of persuasion. Learn to speak vividly; make your words come to life. Inspire Awe in those who hear you. Most people lack vitality of vocabulary - they lack poetry and assuredness. Learn to make your sentences thunder with emotional voltage. Weak or predictable words will cause bright ideas to become dull; it is for the common mind to wallow in the darkness of obscurity.

But powerful words in unusual combinations may illuminate even the darkest corners of a mediocre mind. Make your words shimmer with a most powerful meaning - do not waste a single letter on uncertain or irrelevant statements. Speak with conviction. Create a lightening effect which carries an emotional charge: when the listener is not jolted they are not moved. Words have started wars, and ended them. Words have won the hearts and minds of the masses, and caused them to revolt mercilessly. Words may create love, and choke its life out. Words may bring laughter which lasts a lifetime, or crushing tears which may end a life. Words, when used powerfully, are an incredible ally. A sharp mind is recognized by the words and phrases used, effectively, concisely, and eloquently.

"Use words that are majestic, words that have the power to inflame people's hearts and illuminate their minds."

- Ron. H Williams

Powerful language is specific, and does not rely on scattered generalities and baseless opinion. It is educated, truthful, and logical, leaving little room for argument. Powerful language is substantial, and is remarkable in that truth speaks clearly and effectively, where lies wear thin and lack clarity. There is no better impression than Truth utilized properly and accurately, and no more better effect on ones audience than absolute, unmistakable, evidence.

"Every man is really two men - the man he is and the man he wants to be."

~ William Feather

Powerful language is naturally persuasive. Seek the story that radiates truth and passion for the message you seek to convey. Find the story that is uniquely and wonderfully yours, and tell it to everyone with every ounce of your being. Tell your story with confidence.

Every person has the ability to see with their eyes closed and to hear when there is only silence. They can feel sensations that are not there and taste what they haven't yet eaten. When relating your story, don't speak to the world your customers live in, speak to the world inside their minds. Allow them to experience what you have experienced. Engage the imagination, guide it, and control it. A mind which has followed a story will likely follow with the body as well. People will naturally go to places they have already been in their minds. Allow the listener to become a participant in the story; cause him to perform precisely the action you want them to take in their minds.

There is a dichotomy in communication which must be used by the wise, for matters of clarity, persuasion, and correctness. These two forms of language are logic and emotion. One cannot easily compile an argument based in both, and most cases presented in both manners fail to impress sincerity on the minds of those who have chosen one or the other. Emotional arguments may be planned and presented in a logical manner and achieve both impression and powerful results, but logical arguments become irrelevant under emotional conditions. The Emotional mind and the Intellect are not connected, and process information differently. Humans will often intellectualize emotional decisions in order to justify what "feels" right, without really considering why if feels right in the first place. This is what is often called an "intelligent decision" or a "wise choice".

Words can have a most powerful effect on people, if they are chosen wisely. They can illuminate the mind, enlighten the spirit, win the heart, inspire nobility, and change the world. Learn to speak with poetry - not rhymes and meter, but with elegance and passion.

In Theory and Practice

Fragement of a Serialized Novel

Carl Oliver was prepared for the long walk home, book bag slung loosely over one shoulder, jacket closed against the wet autumn wind. His dormitory was on the far side of campus, past the nursing college, and in sight of the river.

As he drew up to his entrance, he noticed a small package wedged between storm door and the frame. The postage indicated that it was delivered locally, but there was no return address. Strange, he wondered, as he fumbled for his keys, opening the door with a bit of pressure from his foot.

Throwing his jacket against the back of the chair in the common room, he went to the kitchen, prepared a pot of coffee, and settled down at the kitchen table, examining the package. The handwriting was simple, and he didn't recognize it at all. The package measured about six by nine by two - heavy - likely a book. Too solid for a box of chocolates.

Slitting the tape open along the short end, the package fell neatly open, and indeed, a book slipped out, followed by a loose leaf letter, folded neatly in three. The book was untitled, black hard cover, of about two hundred pages. Solid construction - good workmanship - obviously hand made. Opening the book, a brief inscription caught his eye, written in the same simple handwriting:

"I will remember your future,

For it is intertwined with mine.
In Lvx..."

Definitely interesting, to say the least. Opening further, the first chapter began with a beautiful, archaic looking initial.

The Magis

No return mailing address, and definitely not something he'd ordered online. Maybe some kind of prank?

He opened it to the title page, "Magis is a Latin word for "more," and is taken from the motto of the Jesuits, "Ad Majorem Dei Gloriam" which is translated, "For the Greater Glory of God." It is the guiding principle for decision-making for all trained in Ignatian mysticism, one decides in favor of a course of action that is a more than required, and thus, for the greater glory."

His hands slowly dropped to his lap, mind dumbstruck by the connection. This is a book he was promised six years ago, in a time he'd almost forgotten. The signature had changed, but it was sworn to him the day he took an oath, one which he'd forgotten about.

Astrophel Ending

What do you think, that somehow, you can, with the wave of your hand, control the actions of a God? That the story will end or begin at the whim of the characters? You seek power beyond your place, I think. Do you believe that the story will end? And what will happen to you when someone finally reads this story? Will you live again and again, the same life, the same world, with little reconciliation of the fact that you are little more than the words on a page?

The walk up the hill was the loneliest battle ever fought within the mind of a single man. Ever step was that of Abraham and Issac, both who knew something incredible was about to happen. Issac, his throat clenched in anticipation of a vast unknown, but who know that a crescendo was about to be reached. Abraham, who knew only that the time was near when ultimately his loyalty would be tested. For three days neither of them spoke, eating in silence, neither knowing what words to use. Astrophel felt the heavy silence drag upon his every movement, knowing that the time was near where there was no possibility of turning back. This was no whim of the God, an indefinable creator. This was the action of a man, who's own hand was about to control the very actions of his god.

For millennia, he knew, mankind has tried to domesticate their gods, house them in temples, make deals in times of struggle, conveniently forget them in times of plenty. But they did not know what he knew. They did not aspire to become more than what they were. His will was only to become more, to seek beyond.

Decameraton

Note:

The 23 Sin (pronounced SINE) Scripts were written in the years 1999-2000. They were written while in trance, and through a form of automatic writing. These scripts were recorded into the black volume marked on the inside cover "Decameraton", and although there was no name inscribed as to ownership of the volume, the handwriting itself is quite unique, immediately identifying it's author as Frater Perdecertatio.

Sin 00 Chaos Sept.26

A serpent in the eye of every human:
A symbol of the Human Principle,
A representation of our Social Evolution.

Sin 01 Chaos Sept.27

Artifacts and no bones:
The trajectory of artificial sums
And utilitarian friendships
In degrees of random seduction.

Sin 02 Versical Sept 28

Thread of crystal darkness
Glimmering like stars in the night skies.
To those beings gathering here
In the void of the mirrors eye.

Sin 03 Mexa Sept 29

Sex is an art. It is the most intimate form of self-expression
to the person who is your most captive audience. By their
movements you know them.

Sin 04 Versicle Sept 30

What Saint would hide this? Eventual realizations that
sinning can only lead to self-perfection? Somehow,
transcendence awakens an air of evolution.

Sin 05 Versicle Oct 1

What Saint could hide this? Only god's name has changed.
The translation is the switch to dimness ... madness ...
awareness. Give life to that sweet insanity called
enlightenment.

Sin 06 Versicle Oct 4

Awaken where boundries no longer exist: The walls, the
dogs, the security officers of the Priesthood are religion's
true stigmata.

Sin 07 Versicle Oct 5

Among all great masters and messiahs, the great magickians are rare. So often it takes so much physical effort that the display of true Art is the perfection of one's outward being, the glow of a light so profound that it flows outward through the veil of the body. So often it takes so much psychological effort that the display of true Art is Silence. Then, without effort, all effort is gone.

Sin 08 Versicle Oct 18

Reverend Papercut once announced to the world through telepathic suggestion: "Kill the Gods! The rules change under pressure."

Sin 09 Chaos Oct 27

Supplying the future with problems to solve: We've given our children more reasons to hate us than any other generation has ever had.

Sin 10 Versicle Nov 6

Gates of Iron
Spikes and Stone
Walls of Glory
A Fortress called Home.

Sin 11 Versicle Nov 7

People clothed in pale silk, strolling the temple halls in silence. Many sat upon the marble benches while others knelt in meditation or prayer. All wore the same perpetual smile of the divinely deluded: a peaceful countenance of those self assured in their fantasy of certainty and understanding.

Sin 12 Versicle Nov 20

The night air exploded with an eerie blue light, outward from the earth, rendering the darkness with a blinding flash of azure daylight...and as sudden silence penetrated our awareness, it was gone.

Sin 13 Versicle Nov 24

Building a house of cards is harder than letting it fall. There are grains of sand that suddenly slip through our fingers no matter how we grip them, which build castles in the sand which even the quietest of waves could tremble. Even as we struggle against the tide, someday, in this life or another, we will succeed.

Sin 14 Chaos Nov 25

Modern methods of yogic biofeedback: Changing the temperature of the sun by watching a thermometer and changing the color of the night by watching the Sunrise.

Sin 15 Chaos Dec 19

"Life is not always a miracle." Said Omar. The night was clear and cool. The moon shone down across the river's surface, sending flashes of light over the dark reflection of the city.

Sin 16 Versicle Dec 20

I stood overlooking the dell, where moss grew in knots and clumps of lush green amid the dead leaves. Small pools glistened under the dark and rugged trees.

Sin 17 Versicle Dec 21

El Jaharah reached into his pocket and pulled out two polished stones, each the size of a fist. Into his left hand he took the obsidian, leaving the brilliant quartz in his right. Suddenly, he spoke, his voice vibrating the air around us with a power I'd never known could exist in a sound, " We enter here in humility and with the peace of the All Merciful. Let God the Almighty enter into our presence, by the entrance of eternal happiness, of divine prosperity, of perfect joy, and abundant clarity. Let all demons fly from here, and let the angels of peace assist and protect us. Sanctify, Oh God, our humble assembly here, Oh Holy One! Le-Olahm, Amen. "

Sin 18 Versicle Jan 1

Darkness, Limitless and empty. Paradoxially, the abyss I found myself in was both infinitely large and infinitely small. Where there is Nothing to measure there is no volume nor distance to justify dimension. There is no force, and yet the tension is infinite. The silence thundered, roared, and even so, there was no vibration to carry sound. This purity, this finality of senses. And suddenly, LIGHT: Everything at once: BE-ing...Entire universes erupting out of the womb, minds, thoughts, worlds, empires rising and falling, and just as long-lived as the creatures who built them. And then suddenly, it was all gone. Just as quickly and insignificantly as it appeared, it vanished, leaving only the negative image, a memory, on the retina which could not see.

Sin 19 Versicle March 18

If Apostacy were Heretical, then it would be a sin to pray to the God which existed before our conversion, before our baptism, before we ever knew of God. God is neither "All OR Nothing", but "All AND Nothing." All images of God, both in mind and in material are blasphemies to an Eternal Be-ing. God is a Verb.

Sin 20 Chaos March 21

These depths of that knot your belly where the pain of "What Might Be" eventually resides within is called the Mind. There is no Demonic, no Angelic. There only IS. God is not: Thou art God. The Devil is not: Thou art the Devil. Every injustice in the universe is committed by you. Every merciful act of loving-kindness is committed by you. The mind is the most terrible and the most beautiful Be-ing.

Sin 21 Chaos March 28

There is no blasphemy that cannot be justified. You cannot protect the righteous from them-selves. Everyone is guilty of the tragedy of ignorance.

Sin 22 Versicle April 22

I am the god, I am the Priest,
I am the Devil, I am the Beast,
But through it all, Wolf or Lamb:
Only know: I am (that I am).

Sin 23 Versicle April 23

Truth is a matter of perception. All statements are generalities by their very natures. Thus, all truths are going to be false under some circumstances and true in others. If all truths are never full truths, and if a statement is not true, it is by its very nature, false. Therefore, all statements are false.

DECAMERATON

History is written in the sands of the desert. The deserts of the East are the birthing point for the heart of religion of mankind, just as it was the birthing point of man himself. It has always been the way of mankind to attempt at self awakening, self awareness and self perfection. It has always been the weakness of mankind to consider selfishness, materialism, power and tyranny over the enlightenment of himself, his fellow being, and his environment. Every age is a turning point for mankind. Every age offers mankind the chance to awaken, the chance to realize his most perfected self, and to evolve into something much more perfectly human. Very few among us have written into the sand a future history so perfect as our great masters. We must as a species work together to undo the damage done by our forefathers. Every moment I offer you the chance for reconciliation. Each and every one of us has spilled blood upon the earth with our actions, with our desires, with our very presence. None of us are clean. None of us are guiltless. Every moment I offer you forgiveness for the broken covenant our species has openly rejected. Every moment, it is I within You who offers a way towards enlightenment and the ultimate fulfillment of our people: the evolution into something more perfectly human, into the Godlings that we are. Thou art God. Realize your divinity and aspire to it. This may only be done through discipline, and through discipline comes freedom. I have been constantly asked: Who is God? What is God? Where is God? Who speaks for God? And I may only answer that "God Is". God is pure and undifferentiated "Being". Do you not remember the words uttered to Moshe in the desert? "I am that I am." And the words uttered by the Christ? "Thou art God." The attainment of awareness: that is God. The attainment of perfect Karma (action): that is God. The Attainment of Perfect Dharma: that is God.

Kindness is ignored, and looked upon as weakness. Where there is no mercy in the heart of the nations, there is no mercy in the heart of the individual. Where hate and scorn rule the mind, so too must pain and fear rule the soul. And for these numb to divinity, I pray forgiveness. For these deprived of holiness, I pray awareness. One day mankind will awaken, one day, very, very soon. Insha'allah.

All time is in the present. Every great religion has the understanding hidden within its texts that the universe exists only within the "Now". The ego and its limited understanding of linear "time" presents the fallacy that the past has happened and that the future is not yet come. These are inaccurate assumptions of the lesser mind and must be released. Indeed, even the sciences show that this "fact" exists as a constant, except where gravitation proves that where pockets of dense matter exist, time increases. In certain magnetic fields, where gravity is greatest time ceases to exist where simultaneously time exists elsewhere. Time is an irrelevancy.

What we perceive about the past we may also perceive about the future. What we perceive about the future we may also perceive about the past. Time is insubstantial (not intangible as many assume), and it stretches in every direction. It flows according to the same rules and obligations of the mind...in infinite directions and according to the limitations of relative perceptions. The future may be "remembered" in the same manner as the past. The past may be "planned" for just as future events are.

It has been said that the kingdom of God is to be found both within and without you. The magickal definition of time is also to be found within and without you. Without, you may travel and traverse the infinite boundaries of the created universe. Within, you may extend the boundaries of the created universe with the kingdom within you in infinite directions. Thou art God, and in this is a great secret. You too have the ability to create, for we are all existent within the mind of our creator, just as every being we create has the ability to exist within our minds.

There are infinite possible futures, and infinite possible pasts. It is the magickian God within the Mind of man that is the Croix of all and everything. One may speak through the minds of all and everything, of every existent creature, of every atom in the illusion of matter, of every illusion in the mind of Man and of God. There is no I (ego), only I AM (Eheieh).

In this is your Path, whether or not you choose it. It is yours. The universe within and without will follow you until the end of your days in this life, and on into the life in the next. Thou art God, but thou art not GOD. You exist within the mind of God as a co-creator. This discipline, the duty and obligation of every magickian is to perfect thyself, to become worthy of the Ascendancy, to break out of the cycle of reincarnation and to assist others attain the same. "When every Man attains awareness, then the universe will also awaken."

NOTES:

RE: 'Just a little reminder of which side the bread is buttered on':

Who are the people who are making the movement towards solidarity? The ones who really have something to lose when the axe falls. Pagans generally present themselves as people with a cause and a concern towards religious rights and freedoms. The Wiccan movement, based in a "history" of religious intolerance sees the same intolerance within their own system of belief. "Amber K", a renowned Wiccan writer, cannot help but throw an uneducated and negative opinion into everything she writes. Most Pagans come to the path through a Christian background as a rebellion to their parent's fundamentalism or inconsistency. Do children from Pagan families go through a Christian Fundamentalist rebellion too? Time will tell. Which side is the bread buttered on? Who are the people speaking out for YOUR rights and religious freedoms?

The US law states that you may choose your form of worship based on what you feel is correct and accurate. Pagan religions in a historical context have a bloody and powerful history. I understand many people's need to move towards their Pagan roots, but in the pursuit of these they must also remember that whatever form of Divinity they choose to invoke, they must do so in a manner acceptable to that deity. Our present day forms of Paganism are shockingly inaccurate and blasphemous to the Gods we suppose ourselves to worship. Magickal contexts are a much different thing altogether. Magickians and mystics are known to understand divinity from a perspective of Pan-Theos - "All God". We are worshiping God(dess) in whatever form it happens to present itself. As well, we take Jung's and Campbell's concepts as a mythological archetype into consideration. The transmigration of one religion into another's culture is sure to change it. Historically, these religions are inaccurate. Scholars, for example will argue that the Christ myth is a recreation of the Osiris myth. Does this misunderstanding validate blaspheming ones own form of

Divinity? Does accuracy have any place in a religious context?

Where we consider this is in the traditional religions that are still in extent. Judaism is a religion split into several factions of orthodox worship. Many people are lax on their "interpretation", but do not necessarily hold it against each other except where apostasy is concerned. Christianity in its more traditional orthodox forms is also an example of a split religion over "interpretation" and misunderstanding. Islam, the same. Do any of these religions have troubles of accuracy where their "Interpretation" is concerned? Do you remember 9-11? Do you remember the Witch Trials? Do you remember the mass murders of Auschwitz? Do you remember any of the wars fought in the names of Peaceful and Loving Gods?

The closest thing we have to accurate data concerning any historical religious practice is in Anthropology. These do not really consider the rituals and the ideas regarding the ancient religions and cultures we claim to emulate. These people had different ideas, opinions, and cultures than we do today, and a cheap "Genuine – Imitation" religion based on nothing more than mythology is little more than impulsive. Again, I must restate my position: I do not oppose Paganism of the appropriate orthodox forms, with the exception that these died out well over a thousand years ago, and that every modern interpretation is without grounds and tradition. We all create God in our own image, and invoke that which seems most appropriate for us to do so, BUT: this is a sure way to manifest within our own psyche's an imbalance in archetypal force. Invocation of the Perfected Self is the manner which has proven to be of the most efficient and appropriate use of these methods. Anything less is hazardous to the perceptions and the mental balance. Behind the façade that we create with our minds,

God is so much more than we can imagine. To give a name, face, sex or form to IT is a definite limitation of one's perceptions of that infinite be-ing, and so is both an insult and a blasphemy.

"Of course, magick doesn't need to be real for people to believe in it. Any proof – no matter how miniscule, no matter how far removed – will give enough of a fingerhold to attract the weak. It is then, and only then, that you can control them."

- Frater Perdecertatio

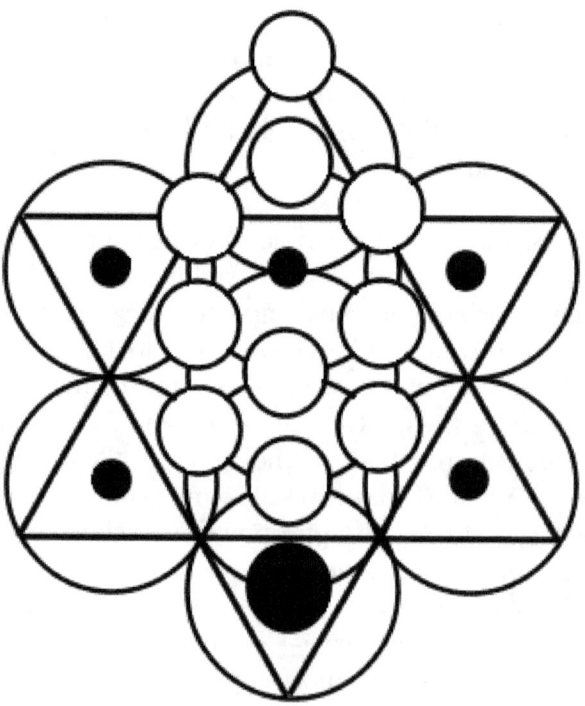

"Even the Kabbalah is an erroneous system which may be warped to suit the needs of those who would seek power, and only those capable of in depth research will ever know the truth – and only then for the lack of any reliable evidence and counter evidence."

– Frater Ego Esse

RE: "...but to make such a generalization that seems rather tunnel vision..."

Indeed, to make any statement at all is a generalization, and there will always be exceptions to any rule: even in something so apparently empirical as mathematics. Truth is a relation that has none. Truth is a theory, nothing more. Every theory is limited by the nature of language to the unfortunate quality of the Labels we choose to assign to an object or behavior in nature. Something rarely happens the same way twice, which is why we have such a difficulty where science is concerned. Magick is a science of reproducible results. Anything less is wishful thinking and what our dear old friend Crowley called "breaks". Most people who practice magick say that it is based on the manipulation of synchronous effects, which does away with any real method of practical application, or any need to justify magick with a scientific explanation. It is both laziness and ignorance. These people I do not consider to be Magickians. They are little more than simple-minded imitators and charlatans. Magick is not for the weak of will, nor the weak of mind. Magick is a specific action performed to create a specific outcome – no matter the method.

We are obsessed by our own under-educated opinions. We rarely look into facts and rarer still do we consider the full significance of the magickal formulae we practice, or not. We are conditioned by western thinking, which is itself affected by Christian thought. We certainly do not think of ourselves as Christians, but every thought is tainted by western Christianity. Regardless of our own education, we are still influenced by the Christian - saturated - society. It is like the communist society which still requires a monetary system to equalize one service for another: one trade becomes as important or as unimportant as any other.

RE: "I am curious of one thing though? Is this the direction the group is going? Towards religious indignation?"

"Religious Indignation: Resentment aroused by unjust, unworthy, or unscrupulous beliefs or observances." Wouldn't you be? Mythology is the basis of religious beliefs, and these in turn are manipulated to have a particular meaning in each individual's observations. I do not know of any Christians who accurately practice Christianity. Just so, I do not know any Pagans who devoutly practice any of the orthodox forms of paganism. Most of us are willing to pick and choose what we practice and follow. The Christians have a saying: "Even the Devil can quote scripture". This means that one may choose to distort the meaning and context of a word or phrase to suit their own purposes. Just so, Pagans will often choose to manipulate their half-formed conceptions to suit their own means. Wicca is one such atrocity.

As to my (often) cynical and sarcastic postscripts, they are not indicative of the direction of the path of the magickian, but are very much the idea of the Elitist Magick board. I have found, over the last few months that this board has been active, that we tend to lose members based on their finding insult in "truth". Their own bias becomes their own justification. This is self-identifying, and therefore ignorant. As such, it can be called "non-elitist". I also wanted to discover how many people were actually paying attention. I fully expected to lose six to seven people due to that particular post, and found it very interesting to discover that we only lost two.

Invocation of the Sub Elementals

Invocation of Air

Air of Air

I invoke you, the vision and ecstasy of universal intelligence; you, who are acquainted with the secret of the harmony of Life; you, whose intimacy is a rose of divine truth! You, whose lips glow with the touch of divine prayer! O Prince of the Chariots of the Winds.

Fire of Air

I invoke you, Citadel of universal and true Faith; you, who exists as a voice of rushing fire; you, who speaks with a thousand whirling winds; for whom wisdom is a universe unto itself, O Lord of Winds and Breezes.

Water of Air

I invoke you, who is a dark and stormy sea of understanding; you, for whom an impression is a complete world; the light of your thought makes clear whatever is obscure, and on your lips is the key to all sacred mysteries, O Queen of the Throne of Air.

Earth of Air

I invoke you, whose wisdom is beyond my understanding, you, who brightens the glass of perception; I am humbled by

192

your look, which turns dust into flames, for you kindle knowledge with the spark of Divine Love, O Princess of the Rushing Winds.

Invocation of Fire

Air of Fire

I invoke you, the soul in the body of the universe; you, who breathes music into the Light of Life; Life envies Death when death is for your sake! I have nourished your flame in my heart, O Prince of the Chariot of Fire.

Fire of Fire

I invoke you, the flame of Gnosis; you, who burns to ashes the Shroud of Ignorance; you, who demands its sacrifice in the name of Wisdom. We are dispersed like stars in the world, O Lord of Flame and Lightning.

Water of Fire

I invoke you, whose blaze enthrones the sun in the sky, and lightning encircles you with adoration for ever; give us the sleepless eye and the passionate heart; be the mirror of mine all-burning love, O Queen of the Thrones of Fire.

Earth of Fire

I invoke you, idol image fired into my mind. I seek the secrets within my Soul. I seek the mysteries of my nature. Once more dwell in our breasts, O Princess of the Shining Flame.

Invocation of Water

Air of Water

I invoke you, protector of the Light of the universe; you, who has filled our glass with the sweet wine of knowledge. The Sun and Moon are bright with your radiance. You have washed from me self conceit and arrogance, O Prince of the Chariot of the Waves.

Fire of Water

I invoke you, oh prison guard of my own mind; you, who have broken loose the wheel of time; you, who acknowledges neither beginning nor end, whose thought is eternal, whose gift is infinitude, O Lord of Waves and the Waters

Water of Water

I invoke you, the conscience hidden in God's heart; you, in whose essence divinity is mirrored. In your womb is built a new world of true Be-ing! You have graced our minds with the gnosis of truth, O Queen of the Thrones of the Water.

Earth of Water

I invoke you, the bright radiance of God's eye; you, who knows that the Sun does not last forever, for who joy and sorrow are nothing; you, who showers with Light the gardens of Life, O Princess of the Waters

Invocation of Earth

Air of Earth

I invoke you, the Heart of Honor and the Glory of Love; you, who causes the beams of true spiritual Light to shine;

you, whose spread lips broke the silence with ecstatic utterance; the great Be-ing who holds influence over sun, moon, and stars, O Prince of the Chariot of Earth.

Fire of Earth

I invoke you, the Fearless Thought which passes beyond Heaven; you, who reconciles Lifelessness with Immortality; you, who fan the Flames of Life with the breath of Gnosis; your perfect understanding and illumination is the Heart of the Mind, O Lord of the Wild and Fertile Land.

Water of Earth

I invoke you, who is the Holy Water of Life; you, who are the Womb of the Earth, regarding yourself as both the clay and the water; you, the granite which floats and the moisture which sinks. Where, in those places where the Sun cannot reach, Darkness is known by another name, O Queen of the Thrones of Earth.

Earth of Earth

I invoke you, O Gate of Truth and Darkness Illuminated; you, who is the Ashes of Existence and Life in Death, for whom the stars keep lit and for whom the Sun rises; the Black Stone becomes a mind of Clearest Diamond, O Princess of Echoing Hills.

Five Years

Lord, It has been five years of Silence. Five years since I have removed myself from your Light in search of my inner truth. Five years of longing and dissatisfaction. Five years of humble learning and purification. I have remedied my sin. I have learned what I needed to learn. I am ready for Initiation, Oh Lord.

I wish to speak the first word of my next prayer of opening to you, Oh Father, Brother, Son, Mother, Sister, Daughter, as you would speak it through me. This has been five years of loneliness, Oh Lord, five years without brothers and sisters to accompany me.

Five years.

"Our thesis carries one obligation, that life is a ceaseless period of transition. We are here for a short, short time, to learn and practice. This thesis is not a work of philosophy, nor of speculation. It is the only truth I know. It is the only reality I have ever experienced. The significance of one's existence is really a simple matter, one which does not require a religious interpretation. Every point made in this essay is clearly identifiable and immediately verifiable in your own experience.

And yet, in order for us to operate effectively, we must embrace life and all it has to offer.

We must learn to let go of our misconceptions, and realize that everything we assume to know is a misconception. This is a world of half truths, generalizations, and lies. We presuppose before we are aware of reality that we are the best judge of what is real and what is not. We must forget all that we know if we are to accept what reality is."

"Oh, but it was you, who in your own uneducated understanding thought that I was the devil, and that you alone knew the truth. And I know that the closest you ever came to truth was the spoon-fed drivel that passes for religion. You don't know, and you'll never know. The devil is your God, and the God that you worship is He that you condemn with every word, with every sermon, with every breath. Yes, even the devil can quote scripture, and you have the Devil in you. My Son, when you look for evil, you will find it everywhere. Not a soul will remain unpainted by your brush. Always has it been like this, always have you lived in a cobwebbed world filled with the horrors of the day, and the terrors of the night. I know you, I have been where you are, but I have had a million lives to realize that."

--Frater Astrophel

The Elitist

I am a magickal elitist. This means that I can only really accept the Adepti in magickal circles. Magick is a place where there exists much theory and opinion, but very little practice and research. Magick is a place where everyone seems to have a personal pet theory.

The people in the magickal circles are of three types of personality: The Elitist(Adept), The Blind Teacher (Babbler), and the Blind Student (Dabbler). The Elitist follows the rules, the traditions, does his homework, practices his rituals, and becomes a fundamentalist only through experience, but not through blind faith. The Blind teacher has given uplooking for the scientific, logical or reasonable path. They have instead chosen those concepts that they like, and discard the rest as unnecessary.(Subsequently, this causes imbalance and weak will.) The Blind Student is unsure of what is within the world of the occult, but has a drive and desire to know. They will learn as much as they can from any source, including inverse and opposing forces such as Christianity and the Blind Teacher. This is a case of the "Blind leading the Blind".

There are of course, the ignorant among us, who choose to blaze their own paths to the goals of the occultists. This is the person who chooses to be "Self-Taught", shunning all concepts but their own. From one such as this I have heard it said, "I believe the universe is shaped like a dough-nut." There was no line of thought, or reasoning behind such conceptions. Their motto is often, "I will go my own way, and make my own mistakes. I don't need a guide, teacher, or tradition to show me the way." Others such as this have said the same, and have become homeless, ignorant, and unintelligent persons of little or no importance in the world, except as a burden to the societies they live amongst.

I will admit, as an elitist, that the path of discipline and practice is a difficult and dangerous, but nowhere near as dangerous as ignorance, denial, delusion or unawareness. Ignorance is what is known as "Throwing the pearls amongst the swine (who, of course, have no understanding)", or "Let those who have ears to hear, let them hear." Denial is where one cannot accept the truth, and is a function of the mind, used to protect its artificial belief systems. Delusion is just as often used, but is the belief that "opinion" is in the eye of the beholder, and is just as real as anything else. Delusive opinions are often found in the same places as denial and ignorance, which (like in the Christian system) creates a self-supporting delusion, from which there is no escape (The more one tries to make a person who is deluding themselves understand their predicament, the tighter the delusion becomes). Unawareness, though often mistaken for Ignorance, is not the same. Unawareness is simply the unknown. It is a place that the mind has no vocabulary to describe, and is totally alien to the mind it speaks to (try to describe to a desert dweller the concept of "Ocean" and he will have NO awareness of what you are talking about). Awareness is also the "awakened state " of enlightenment, which is to be fully conscious of the moment, and to be concentrating on the experience of what is happening now, than to be worrying about the future, or dwelling upon the past.

The questions one must ask when studying a system of magick (or any subject, for that matter) are: "Can I accept the possibility that I am wrong? Am I able to change my curriculum based on this possibility?"

A further question to ask is, does the philosophy have a stable foundation? I can argue a priest out of his religion quite simply based on the inaccuracies of his translations. But many pagans, Christians, and other such professed students of mysticism merely accept what they are told based on faith, which is merely the ability to believe in something without proof. A magickian once said that faith is the task of "Believing the unbelievable; seeing the true as the false, and the false as the true; and knowing that what cannot be accepted logically by the adept can be fully accepted by the inept."

Mary

The daughters of a magickian are not as human as they at first appear. This is my first daughter. Her name is Mary. She was stillborn, due to a high content of morphine in her bloodstream.

I live in a world of magick. I live in a universe where my wishes don't always come true, but those miracles that I have a hand in are great ones.

When Mary was born, her mother decided that, despite warnings to the contrary, she would try the drugs they offered her. She did not take into consideration that she was not the only person taking the drugs, and that our daughter was also taking them. Morphine was not intended for babies. She was born dead. Her heart was not beating. Her breath of life was not in her lungs. Within a moment, I knew. Within seconds, I knew that she was not with us. It was then that I performed our greatest magick, the Vault of the Angilluminati. The ritual which may have taken hours in normal time took me but a few seconds. Upon its completion, the baby cried out, and her heart beat as normal.

To this day, she is a blessed child. She is much more intelligent and creative than other children her age. She is strong and independent. She is magickal, as is her older brother, her step mother, and her father. She is a child of love, and a world of peace. Our children are the future. Let us make their lives the miracle that they deserve.

"I am intelligent enough to know that I do not know enough. I am intelligent enough to study those things that most people never find, or never know any more than the trivial rumors. I am intelligent enough to know that I am in no position except that of the magickal chaotic equation of the Lorenz Theorem...I do not count except as a breath. I am intelligent enough to know that my thoughts, so small and beautiful, are like thundering magnificence across the skies of the minds of mankind. I am intelligent enough to know that I see things differently than most people, and these manners of perception most people find insignificant. Did the Buddha know this? Did it ache in his heart to know that he was between common human comprehension and illumination? Is that luminescence beyond me? Will I only ever be a monkey with a ruler and a compass? Will I ever evolve into a true human, the perfected self, above and beyond simple human frailty? My gods, I do not see anything but the seams in reality. I look into a subject beyond the trivial pillow-casings and find the stuffing within. I break past the point of understanding and see that it is only feathers.

What do I wish for? I can already model complex equivalents with a simple rule of thumb. I wish to manifest an incredible genius. If I am a simple man with a simple mind, I wish to accomplish the grandest accomplishment of them all....the grand design...the great and noble Truths behind the simple noble truths. I wish to acquire ascension through genius. I have all that I want. I wish for so much more, and I know how to acquire it. What is beyond my sight?"

--Frater Ego Esse.

TIME

All time is in the present. Every great religion has the understanding hidden within its texts that the universe exists only within the "Now". The ego and its limited understanding of linear "time" presents the fallacy that the past has happened and that the future is not yet come. These are inaccurate assumptions of the lesser mind and must be released. Indeed, even the sciences show that this "fact" exists as a constant, except where gravitation proves that where pockets of dense matter exist, time increases. In certain magnetic fields, where gravity is greatest time ceases to exist where simultaneously time exists elsewhere. What does this mean for the magickian? Simply that time is an irrelevancy.

What we perceive about the past we may also perceive about the future. What we perceive about the future we may also perceive about the past. Time is insubstantial (not intangible as many assume), and it stretches in every direction. It flows according to the same rules and obligations of the mind...in infinite directions and according to the limitations of relative perceptions. The future may be "remembered" in the same manner as the past. The past may be "planned" for just as future events are.

It has been said that the kingdom of God is to be found both within and without you. The magickal definition of time is also to be found within and without you. Without, you may travel and traverse the infinite boundaries of the created universe. Within, you may extend the boundaries of the created universe with the kingdom within you in infinite directions. Thou art God, and in this is a great secret. You too have the ability to create, for we are all existent within the mind of our creator, just as every being we create has the ability to exist within our minds.

There are infinite possible futures, and infinite possible pasts. It is the magickian God within the Mind of man that is the Croix of all and everything. One may speak through the minds of all and everything, of every existent creature, of every atom in the illusion of matter, of every illusion in the mind of Man and of God. There is no I (ego), only I AM (Eheieh).

In this is your Path, whether or not you choose it. It is yours. The universe within and without will follow you until the end of your days in this life, and on into the life in the next. Thou art God, but thou art not GOD. You exist within the mind of God as a co-creator. This discipline, the duty and obligation of every magickian is to perfect thyself, to become worthy of the Ascendancy, to break out of the cycle of reincarnation and to assist others attain the same. "When every Man attains awareness, then the universe will also awaken."

-- Frater Ego Esse, June 26, 2003